WHEN THE WOMAN ABUSED WAS YOU

A Guide to Healing from Childhood Sexual Abuse

DAWN SCOTT DAMON

credo
house publishers

When the Woman Abused Was You

Copyright © 2017 Dawn Scott Damon

Published in the United States by Credo House Publishers,
a division of Credo Communications, LLC, Grand Rapids, Michigan
www.credohousepublishers.com

Scripture taken from the Holy Bible, New International Version™ NIV.
Copyright © 1973, 1978, 1984, 2011 by Biblica. Used by permission of Zondervan.
All rights reserved worldwide.

ISBN: 978-1-625860-76-7

Cover and interior design by Sharon VanLoozenoord
Editing by Donna Huisjen

Printed in the United States of America

First edition

— Contents —

Part 4: DANCING IN TRIUMPH

Finding the Free after Healing

— Let's Get Started —

We are survivors, you and I. We have experienced one of life's most personal violations: sexual abuse. We feel alone, shamed—and at times desolate. Our victimization has jaded the way we view and feel everything. When we can actually feel, that is. Our journey starts here—together. I've stood where you are standing. At the starting point of what feels like an impossible journey.

That's why I'm going to walk this healing path with you—to help you discover that healing is possible, and that it's most certain if you take these steps. Sexual abuse and trauma may be a part of your history, but abuse doesn't have to define who you are or restrict you from living an amazing life.

You're already off to a good start by picking up this healing tool. Reading this book will change the trajectory of your life and give you the confidence you need to get unstuck and move forward. My good friend Deborah Jo says, "Whenever I'm struggling with something, I drive to my favorite bookstore, walk in the front door and head straight to the 'HELP!' section." Congratulations—you've found help.

So, together we journey.

◆　◆　◆

Before I started my healing journey, I didn't wake up each day with an awareness of my abusive past, nor did I experience a daily, traumatic reliving of events, but the disfigurement of abuse did stare back at me in the mirror. As with the Peanuts character Pig Pen, a sense of "dirty" hovered around me like a dust mist, polluting my senses with victim messages. I was suffocating under a haze of shame and weary of a life weighted down by the chains of my sexual abuse.

I wanted more. I prayed for more.

My pastor's wife offered me an invitation to a women's study, and I joined a support group for survivors. I was terrified to participate, but I was equally terrified to remain the same. I'd made a decision to heal, and I was ready to shake off Pig Pen's dust, face the woman in the mirror, and take back control of my life.

That decision hadn't come to me easily, and it definitely didn't come overnight—it was fourteen years in the making, actually. But my choice to heal was the beginning of a new life. Healing is an ongoing process that culminates when we reach heaven, and today I can confidently say that I'm *mostly* healed! I'm thankful that I accepted my pastor's wife's invitation and so very grateful she reached out to me, even when I was far-from-approachable, if you catch my drift.

If the scars of your past have left you emotionally disfigured and you're ready to look in the mirror, know that your life can change. Your future doesn't have to be defined by past sexual abuse. Like me, you're a woman who has chosen to step into the life God intended for you to live.

Right now, I'm extending an invitation to you. I want to walk beside you as you shed the old abuse victim identity and claim a new beginning. I'll help you understand the aftermath of sexual abuse and enter into cleansing, healing waters.

You've lived a confused, cold, and shamed life long enough.

It's time for *you* to reclaim what was stolen—your energy, joy, and freedom.

Choose Life

Healing is possible. A fresh beginning beckons you. But change won't come magically.

In the Scriptures God shows us an important life principle: the power of choosing: "Today I have given you the choice between life and death, between blessings and curses. I call on heaven and earth to witness the choice you make. Oh, that you would choose life, that you and your descendants might live!" (Deuteronomy 30:19, TLB).

God lays two paths before His people.

One way leads to life. More than to mere existence, *life* refers to peace, tranquility, prosperity, and safety. The path of life isn't only for God's children but also for their children and grandchildren. The implications of the power of choice can't be overestimated. Deuteronomy 30:19 implies that our choices and subsequent lifestyle consequences are passed down to our future generations.

The other choice referred to in this verse leads to death and destruction, a path marked by hardship and obstacles. God allows us to make our own choices. While He longs for us to flourish and thrive, He permits us the freedom to make our own decisions.

Likewise, healing is a choice. When you decide you want to heal—a decision you'll have to reaffirm throughout your journey—you choose life—to live in freedom and fullness. Your commitment will also help you stay focused and empower you to *endure the process*, because *healing is a process*—a twisting, turning trail marked by ups and downs, ins and outs.

The choice to heal isn't a one-time decision.

Only you have the power to choose to heal. Only you can determine how quickly or slowly you will walk the healing path. If you choose, you can at any point set down this book and take a break, then pick it back up and continue when you feel ready.

The journey will be difficult, but you're strong enough to take it and make it—much stronger than you think.

You know it's time.

Time to stop cowering in the threatening shadow of abuse. Recovery is a difficult process, but as I look back on my own healing season I can honestly say it was the sweetest pain I've ever known. Because on the road to recovery I met Jesus in new and powerful ways. He will walk beside you, too, if you just ask Him.

In fact, He's waiting for you to make that invitation right now.

Help for the Journey

You're about to embark on an amazing journey. I'd like to offer a few suggestions to help you along the way:

+ Pause at the Roadside Check-up and consider the reflective questions. These questions are designed to insert *you*, your self—and your distinctive emotions and perceptions—into the story, so that you remain *present* and *connected* as you read.

+ Answer the questions in writing. As we activate our brains through the exercise of writing, we validate the answers we might otherwise have considered tentative or vague, unleashing the tethered places of our hearts.

+ Other survivor sisters are praying for you—women who, just like you, are pursuing wholeness. Welcome. So when I use the word *we*, remember the women who have traveled this path before you who are cheering you on. Together we can make it. Join us at freedomgirlsisterhood .com for more info.

+ My words are meant to inspire you to reach for God's best. As your coach and cheerleader, my voice will at times be motivational and challenging. Don't allow yourself to feel intimidated. Don't give up and opt out. At other times my tone will comfort and give you permission to feel those painful emotions you've worked so hard to mask and squelch. Know that my words are always intended to be supportive and validating because I believe in you and in this life-changing journey on which you're embarking. You go, girl!

+ No two people's experiences are exactly the same. Your story is your own, and you're the only one who can define how traumatic it was. Your pain is valid.

+ Everyone responds to abuse differently, and no response is right or wrong. Many factors—varied and unique—shape a survivor's response. *Your responses—whatever they may be—are authentic and valid.*

+ Healing is a process, not an event or a destination. Recovery is a journey, and you'll travel the road in your own way and at your own speed. *Your process is valid.*

Congratulations. You're about to begin a journey that will change your life forever.

— *Part 1* —

DEFINING THE TRAUMA

Exploring the Painful Events of Your Story

The most beautiful people we have known are those who have known defeat, known suffering, known struggle, known loss, and have found their way out of the depths. These persons have an appreciation, a sensitivity, and an understanding of life that fills them with compassion, gentleness, and a deep loving concern. Beautiful people do not just happen. —ELISABETH KUBLER-ROSS

COMING OUT OF THE FOG
Releasing Denial and Accepting Your Story

Once you start recognizing the truth of your story, finish the story. It happened but you're still here, you're still capable, powerful, You're not your circumstance. It happened and you made it through. You're still fully equipped with every single tool you need to fulfill your purpose.
—STEVE MARABOLI

Let the Healing Begin

Facing your story can be overwhelming.

The emotions that accompany recall and recovery from abuse are as intense and unpredictable as the dips and turns of a rollercoaster. Processing the past is hard work physically, mentally, and emotionally. Physical symptoms often disrupt life. You may feel mentally exhausted. These and other symptoms that are part of recovery can threaten your resolve to continue.

Sadly, many survivors never reach out for help and remain paralyzed by the past. Gripped by fear and denial, those who decline to walk toward healing often remain locked within the dark cell of the past.

But you've chosen to pick up this book. In taking this seemingly insignificant step you've demonstrated incredible courage. This single step suggests that you see the vast chasm between where you are and where you want to be.

You desire something more for your life. Something better.

You can live this "better," blessed life. I believe that "better" is not only possible for your life—it's within your grasp. Life—real, authentic, full living—exists after abuse. Healing and wholeness can be yours. Don't let fear rob you of future hope any longer.

You're a survivor—strong beyond your wildest dreams.

You're an overcomer. You've endured the horrific—yet you're still standing, still breathing, still reaching, and even daring to experiment with hope.

You're ready for change, desperate for a new reality.

Your new life begins—

one

step

at a time.

Small Steps

Choosing to read this book is your first step in *acknowledging* your readiness to face your story and find help for healing.

You're taking that all-important first step: acknowledging. You know well enough that something isn't right deep inside you. That something about your life needs to change. Write down those feelings of acknowledgement in the space provided here. This may be something as honestly simple as this: "I recognize that sexual abuse has stolen from me and victimized me. Harmful consequences are robbing me of a healthy and happy life. Today I am ready to face the reality of my abuse and start my journey toward healing."

Congratulations! This is precisely the way in which most of us find healing—one tiny, essential step after another.

Maintaining forward momentum is important—even (and perhaps especially) when the process is painful and messy. Every step is another blow to stubborn strongholds linked to your past.

Small steps don't make *a* difference—they make *all* the difference.

◆　◆　◆

My Story

I'm a survivor of childhood sexual abuse. I'm telling my story because I believe it will help you find comfort and insight in the understanding that you aren't alone.

I stumbled my way to healing because of God's faithfulness. I wish someone had helped me process the effects of my abuse much earlier in my life. I was young and alone when I discovered the connection between the deep shame, guilt, anger, and rage I was experiencing and my childhood sexual abuse. Those emotions grew inside me for years because I didn't know how to go about searching for freedom.

My story can be a tool to empower you to reach for healing and help on your journey.

My Memories

God may be protecting me, but I don't have total recall of my abuse; however, my vivid, disconnected memories tell me with certainty that I was sexually molested as a child. I can't tell you when it began or how many years it lasted. Until a few years ago I couldn't even have told you how my abuse affected me.

But I can tell you who the perpetrator was.

For the first years of my childhood I was a happy kid, free and innocent. I'm thankful for those sweet, formative years. This backdrop of early love instilled in me positive self-esteem and gave me a solid start. Yet behind a curtain of love and protection lurked a monster—a sexual predator.

My dad by day and my abuser by night.

I don't remember the first time my father sexually assaulted me, how it started, or how old I was. I have only jumbled memories. One night I went to bed with a child's innocence, and the next morning I awakened with intense shame. My father, my childhood hero, had become my abuser.

Although I can't recall that first experience, I recollect snippets of other incidents far too vividly.

Later, when I became an adult, I was acutely aware of my desire for the hemorrhage inside me to be stanched. I just didn't know how to make that happen. Year by year my confidence, purpose, and hope withered as I helplessly watched the consequences inexorably unfolding:

My marriage fell apart.

My health deteriorated.

My emotional well-being tanked.

I was miserable.

My ongoing connection to God was one of the few things I had going for me. I somehow managed to eke out a simple prayer: "God, I long to be whole. Do surgery on my heart, wash my mind, and heal me from my past." Until that time I hadn't read the Bible on my own or given its words much consideration, but that day I reached for one of my high school graduation gifts—a Bible—and "happened upon" these incredible words: "The LORD will guide you always; he will satisfy your needs in a sun-scorched land and will strengthen your frame. You will be like a well-watered garden, like a spring whose waters never fail" (Isaiah 58:11).

Those words rang in my heart as a personal, exclusive promise from God, and they remain my promise today. I've clung to them in dry times. I've recited them when my frame was feeling crushed. I've mouthed them when I was lost and needed direction.

On the very day I claimed the promise of Isaiah 58:11 my healing began—because I had made a choice. God had given me a picture of who I was and of what I could and would become in Him.

The Choice to Heal

This may sound counterintuitive, but the truth is that making the choice to heal can be frightening. Choosing to heal implies that you're willing to cleanse the wound—and that means that you'll have to touch it or allow it to be touched. It means that you're willing to come out of hiding, to feel, to lay down your well-used weapons of survival.

Choosing to pursue healing means being willing to change, and change can feel desperately frightening. Your pain came in the first place because someone else took control of your life. So giving up your carefully guarded self-management means facing more vulnerability to hurt. The last thing you want to do is feel uncomfortable, afraid, and defenseless again.

Choosing to heal, however, is really a decision to *let God take control.* And if your relationship with Him hasn't been distorted by negative associations, giving God control won't leave you exposed, powerless, and open to victimization. On the contrary, letting go of control (an illusion because none of us truly controls our life) means being willing to drop your defense mechanisms—a necessary first step toward becoming stronger than ever. Strength equals empowerment, and empowerment makes us healthy. Bravado is a façade—a false image of who we really are.

Choosing to heal doesn't reduce us to frail, spineless women. Quite to the contrary, our decision to rid ourselves of the ghosts of our past is an act of courage requiring a degree of strength we can only—and rightly—define as superhuman.

Some survivors never make it this far.

You're different.

You've already taken that giant first step of opening—and beginning to read—this book. Making the decision to heal is the best choice you can make. Learn to love yourself. God has a brilliant future for you.

If you feel you aren't ready, I understand.

But remember, indecision is itself a decision—a decision to stay stuck. Unwell. Chained to the past.

◆　◆　◆

Potholes on the Road to Recovery

The healing journey doesn't take us to Disneyland, but neither is it a pointless, short-lived, circular ride to nowhere. Far from being a jarring, excruciating experience, it may be described, particularly in hindsight, as a fluid, flowing process of reclaiming our God-created identity as we learn to walk in freedom. It's an exciting journey of discovery—but that doesn't mean it's easy. The road we travel, while it has its smoother stretches, is riddled with potholes, including fear, pride, and negativity.

The Pothole of Fear

"I'm afraid that if I start feeling I'll fall into a deep, dark hole and never get out," I told my counselor the day my long-frozen emotions started to thaw. I'd clung long and hard to my theory (which had served me quite nicely, I might add) that crying opened the door to feelings, which in turn led to weakness—which ultimately cracked open the gateway to pain. Crying was the recourse of weaklings and babies, not of women who knew better than to believe in childhood fantasies and happy-ever-afters.

Yet I was on the verge of being inundated by a veritable tsunami of tears. My counselor had nearly dug her way through my emotional levee, and my grief, pain, and anguish were ready to burst through.

"Let yourself go and feel what you're feeling, Dawn. You'll be freer than you've ever been."

Her encouragement afforded me the courage and permission I needed to experience the deep grief I'd bottled up inside me for years.

Buoyed by her invitation, I allowed my feelings to surface, even though I faced intense fear. I discovered to my surprise, however, that my fear of my feelings was actually much greater than the discomfort of the feelings themselves. For years I'd been running from an illusion.

Fear is common to survivors. Perhaps some of the following common survivor fears resonate with you:

Fear of Going Insane

We sometimes feel as though we're one . . . "something" away from losing it. One memory, one heartache, one tear away from total breakdown. We worry that if we allow ourselves to turn around and backtrack into our pain we "won't be able to function," that we'll "break down and won't be able to be a good mother [fill in another role if it fits better]" or that "I'll lose my job, my husband, my world." Our fear is real enough; what we don't realize is that most of the consequences we fear are not.

While it's certain this journey will stir up your emotional pot, the process will leave you stronger, better blended, and richer not weaker. Face the fear and tell anxiety "You aren't going to win," and you'll make it through the storm to discover the calm.

Fear of Losing a Relationship

"People won't love me if they find out what I've been through." "He'll think I'm damaged goods."

Losing a relationship or being abandoned is possible. But how likely are these outcomes to occur? Have your past relationships been turbulent or volatile? Shallow or void of true intimacy? Have they been plagued by compromised truth, peppered with fights, infidelities, and false hopes? If you remain wounded and unhealthy, you could lose the hope of real, deep, and intimate relationships altogether.

Anyone you allow into your life should truly love you for who you are and should be your number one champion in healing. Reject the fear of abandonment. Make a decision to take the journey with or without support—because it's time for you to fight for a healthy you.

Fear of Facing the Truth

"I'm not really that deeply affected. I'm over it. I forgave, so it doesn't matter anymore. He or she died, so it's too late anyway."

Someone once observed that "denial is a beautiful thing." And I agree—it is beautiful, provisionally and for the briefest of moments. Then it turns around and strikes like a snake, leaving us to cope with a lethal dose of venom.

Ignoring the truth is never a replacement for authentic healing. Ignorance is far from bliss when it comes to the deep gashes of the soul. The aftermath of sexual assault, left unattended, is a slow hemorrhage that leads eventually to emotional death. Yet many survivors don't want to face the truth, fearing that the truth will expose an even more dire reality:

+ What if they never really loved me in the first place?
+ What if I liked it? Wouldn't that make me the guilty one?
+ I've always secretly believed it was my fault. That feeling had to come from somewhere.
+ I'm worthless, damaged, pitiful. I don't deserve success or happiness.
+ What if being broken is all I'll ever know? What will I do? How will I get the attention I so badly crave?
+ How will I survive if I lose my coping skills?

Stop living in denial. Embrace truth, and go with the self-talk it inspires: "I will honestly look at my past. With God, I can handle whatever I find."

When we confront fear we discover that whatever it is we dread is either a lie or, at the very most, less significant and more manageable than we had imagined.

Fear of Feeling Emotions

You've lived for a long time subconsciously avoiding—by conveniently stuffing—your emotions. In fact, for most survivors emotional repression becomes second nature. That's because it works. Children aren't equipped to either interpret or process the overwhelming feelings that come with abuse: pain, rage, fear, bewilderment, guilt, shame, and even ambivalent pleasure (this last one can be dicey). Their emotional circuitry becomes quickly overloaded. Child victims in particular learn to emotionally numb out in order to survive.

Perhaps you, like me, grew up disconnected from your feelings. I found it necessary to emotionally anesthetize myself to endure certain aspects of the abuse experience. While I instinctively disconnected myself from painful feelings, I wanted to enjoy pleasurable emotions. Yet since it was impossible for me to selectively cut off my emotions, I became numb to *all* feelings, including pleasant and exhilarating ones.

I had to learn to embrace my feelings in order to regain the full range of my emotions. Today I *can feel*, and I enjoy both freedom and wholeness. Your healing will be marked by newfound freedom and emotional release, too. But first you must be willing to do some hard work:

Refuse suppression.

Remain emotionally engaged so you can "thaw out" from your frozen state.

Don't let the fear of feeling stop you.

Once buried emotions surface, tears, upheavals, outbursts, and over-reactions may break loose along with them. That's okay for now. Face your feelings—the whole package. Then sort them out and begin to work through them. As you start to experience feelings once again, the intensity of emotions and their related side effects usually lessens.

Fear of Losing Control

Your abuser violated your boundaries, stripped you of control, robbed you of your voice, and snatched away any autonomy or power. Your world careened out of control, and your circumstances felt scary and chaotic.

You learned to claw your way back to what felt like a position of power in a desperate attempt to maintain, or regain, sanity.

Taking back power made sense. Anyone in your position would have made the same choice.

"I admit it. I'm a control freak," Iris stated flatly. "But what's so bad about that? I like knowing what's going to happen next."

Needing to wrest back a sense of control is a hallmark of women with frightening and tumultuous childhoods. The response feels logical—but in reality our desire to protect ourselves through control is an illusion. We believe that we're impervious to pain as long as we can "keep it all together."

Ironically, though, in order to truly experience healing we have to do precisely the opposite: allow ourselves to take risks and surrender control.

Eventually you'll face these choices.

I know—this will make you feel dangerously vulnerable, but that's the paradox. When you *feel out of control* but still will yourself to let down your defenses, you discover that you're healthier than you could ever have thought possible. This is the moment healing begins.

If you've experienced any or all of the above fears, find a trusted ally to walk and talk with you as you navigate through them. Don't try to take these steps alone.

The Pothole of Pride

Pride hinders us from healing. It blinds us to our true condition and keeps us from admitting, "I have a problem. I need help." You resist the help you need because you don't want to be known as a "survivor of sexual abuse" by the people you care about or want to impress.

But you're only hurting yourself.

Pride may be defined as a stubborn reluctance to deal with the past, preferring to be seen by others as someone who "has it all together." Truth is, though, that you won't find true healing until your pride has been broken. That's because honest and deep healing requires God, and while even God can't penetrate the defenses of the willfully proud, He runs, rejoicing, to the side of the willingly humble.

And what He gives in love will be infinitely superior to anything else you may have been seeking. The Bible is clear that "God goes against the willful proud; God gives grace to the willing humble" (James 4:6, MSG).

Pride says things like:

+ I'm not the one with the problem—you are.
+ I'm fine. I don't need any help.
+ I'm never going to break down.
+ I won't give anyone the satisfaction of seeing me as weak.
+ I refuse to cry—tears are for wimps.

Pride produces false assumptions and fake emotions, like:

+ Control feels energizing.
+ Manipulating people feels good.
+ Denying myself feels powerful. I don't need food, fun, tears, laughter, or any of the other things most people feel are essential to life.
+ It feels safer not to trust anyone. I'll never tell my secret.

The Pothole of Negative Attitude

If you don't like something, change it; if you can't change it, change the way you think about it. —MARY ENGELBREIT

You're staking your claim and building the supporting foundation for a new life. Along the way you're going to experience conflicting emotions. You'll be temped to return to former ways of thinking and living; this is really a return to a victim mindset—living by default instead of by design.

The key to changing your life is changing your attitude.

A positive, God-centered outlook is a powerful tool that will serve you well as you face the aftermath of sexual abuse. Your outlook is your choice. You get to exert healthy self-control by choosing the attitude you'll embrace every day. Refuse to think like a victim. Initiate a winning attitude that empowers you with a strong offense to defeat the "negative-thought saboteurs" you'll encounter on this journey.

Negative-Thought Saboteurs:

Taken alphabetically, these cons include anger, apathy, blame, criticism, cynicism, depression, dishonesty, fear, guardedness, hatred, indifference, intolerance, irresponsibility, jealousy, lack of emotion, mistrust, pessimism, pride, resentment, revenge, sadness, self-pity, shame, skepticism, suspicion, and a victim mentality.

These negative-thought saboteurs impede your success. They're roadblocks, consigning you to a constricted, limiting future.

On your journey to wholeness you'll no doubt uncover hidden and painful memories as you scrabble through the debris of your past. When this happens, contrary to your instincts allow yourself to feel and to experience. Embrace your emotions. But remember to choose an attitude that advances your spiritual, physical, and emotional health. You can say "I hate my life" or "this is stupid." Or you can take the longer view and assert, "I'm going to be free" and even "This is an important part of the process for me."

You choose.

The motivational speaker and author of *Your Erroneous Zones* (1976), Dr. Wayne Dyer states it simply: "If you change the way you look at things, the things you look at change."

◆ ◆ ◆

You're on your way. Your life will never again be the same.

Summing it all up, friends, I'd say you'll do best by filling your minds and meditating on things true, noble, reputable, authentic, compelling, gracious—the best, not the worst; the beautiful, not the ugly; things to praise, not things to curse.
—PHILIPPIANS 4:8, MSG

Roadside Check-up

1. Have you prepared your mind for healing? In what ways?

2. Take a moment to write down ways in which you expect your life to be different once you experience freedom and recovery from the trauma of sexual abuse.

3. Is the healing journey worth taking if it means that you can reach the freedom you've envisioned? If your answer is yes, your mind is prepared. You're ready to begin.

4. If your answer is no, take a moment to pray about it, perhaps using these words: "God, I humble myself before you today and ask you to prepare me for a new life. I surrender my fears, my pride, and my negative attitude to you. I choose to renew my mind and to change the way I view recovery. With the help of your Holy Spirit I will begin this process and be transformed. In Jesus' name, Amen."

Telling Myself My Story

"Why won't she tell me the details?" Frank shook his head in frustration, revealing a broken heart and a wounded ego.

"Frank, your wife won't even tell herself her story. She's spent the last twenty years trying to erase her abuse from her mind, and she's convinced herself that it wasn't real. She's living in denial, a fantasy world. She's telling herself, 'You made this all up. It's just some demented nightmare.' Give her time to tell herself the truth. Then, when she feels safe, she may choose to tell you."

A light came on in Frank's eyes. Suddenly, his wife's behavior seemed to make sense.

Many women who've experienced abuse never tell anyone about their trauma. If and when they do talk, it's usually many, many years after the abuse took place. Only a few people may ever hear the details of a survivor's childhood.

My Story

I began revealing my story by inserting tidbits of disclosure into my talks when speaking to women's groups. This was my unique, controlled way of shattering the silence I'd kept for years, while encouraging other survivors to do the same. On one such occasion, while ministering in Dallas to women on a spiritual retreat, I delicately slipped in a piece of my abuse story. I was in mid-sentence when a woman in her nineties suddenly erupted in repentant shrieks, "It wasn't my fault! I didn't mean to be bad. I didn't know what to do."

The scene was gut wrenching. This precious woman had evidently never before released her story, but that day, in that inadvertently public setting, she let it all out. When she was done crying she literally giggled with joy. She'd been set free. This anecdote showcases the incredible power of "telling." That tidbit from my own story broke loose the secret shame and lies that had held a stranger captive and helped her find freedom in the truth of who and Whose she was.

❖   ❖   ❖

Have you told *yourself* your whole story? Giving words to your experience and pain will crack the emotional safe that's been holding your trauma.

I want to encourage you to try something that might feel risky but promises to be liberating. Jesus tells us, "Then you will know the truth, and the truth will set you free" (John 8:32). As you tell yourself your story, you'll experience freedom. Many survivors live in fear of their own stories. They believe the details to be so appalling that they try to brush over the whole event. As I used to say, "Hey I know it happened, and that's enough." To me, retelling was like dragging the river: when you've already found the body, further searching seems pointless. Even through my self-defensive sarcasm I can hear the agony in my choice of associations: a *body*, *death*, *pain*.

I was trying to run from the brutal reality. My innocence had died—snuffed out at the hands of my father. I'd lost my carefree childhood, and nothing in me wanted to revisit my despicable past. But emotional fragments of my soul were trapped in the chapters of my story. Clues to why I felt the way I did and why I, still today, respond, think, and behave in certain ways. If I hadn't discovered those important pieces of evidence, I wouldn't have fully comprehended the severity of the offenses against me.

Perhaps you've tried to minimize your pain, too.

As you begin to tell your story, blocked out pieces of your past may surface. That's okay—it's to be expected. Fear is part of this experience, but it doesn't have to remain that way forever. Once you face your fear it loses its power to hold you hostage. You're no longer a victim—helpless and hopeless.

You have become stronger than your fear.

You have begun to reclaim the shattered, encapsulated pieces of your soul.

Walls and Masks

Dottie lived for years behind the mask of a self-confident, outgoing professional. Even her heavy make-up hid her true radiance. But behind closed doors with me she lowered her mask to let me glimpse a fragile, broken woman. After one particular conversation Dottie braved the unknown and agreed to begin counseling, and during the process she shared her story. As she worked through the bitter details of how she had been raped as a child by three neighborhood boys, tears traced uneven rivulets through the thick powder foundation that encased her cheeks.

I gasped, "Dottie, you're losing your mask! Jesus is setting you free!" As she shed healing tears, her thick make-up dissolved, revealing glowing skin. Her mask was visibly crumbling as she released years of shame and pain.

The Power of Story

Marketers demonstrate for us that power exists in telling authentic stories. Each of us tells ourselves, and others, a selective narrative about our lives—often focusing on our successes, our goals, and our dreams. Stories help us make sense of things. People crave, and need, some theory or conclusion about the significance of their lives, events, relationships, etc.

The story you tell to and about yourself carries incredible impact. But have you been telling an authentic, inclusive, comprehensive story? Have you been telling the truth—the whole truth, and nothing but the truth—about yourself?

Many abuse survivors have difficulty relating authentic self-narratives because they're disconnected from their own emotions and intuition. It has become hard for them to distinguish between the historical facts of their lives and their emotional aftermath.

However, our stories ignite our passion. The things that happen to us naturally evoke an emotional response. When you tell yourself your authentic story, you re-connect with your heart. Your story has the power to reawaken dormant emotions. Once you can understand the historical facts of your story and can relate it to the resulting emotions, healing can begin.

Your story belongs to you, but God holds the next chapter in His hands. He's the author, and if you let Him He'll arrange even the painful parts into something beautiful. God will redeem the sad and tear-stained pages of your life's manuscript; only He can promise a glorious ending.

◆　◆　◆

Roadside Check-up

It's your turn to tell your story—to *yourself*. Begin in this way:

1. Just the Facts, Ma'am

Tell the facts of your story—the *who, what, where, when,* and *how* of your abuse experience. This is the *intellectual or historical* version of your story.

Relating the intellectual or historical version helps you get comfortable with remembering, admitting, and accepting what happened to you. Tell as much as you can remember with as much detail as possible. Write down your story, and then read it back, aloud, to yourself. Talk into a recorder, speak to a chair, or address your own image in a mirror. The goal at this stage is to report events, not engage with emotions.

In the reporting stage, you relate a factual account of the events without judgment, criticism, denial, justification, or reasoning. Avoid focusing on the consequences, including the pain, hurt, and anger you felt. Just lay out the facts as accurately and completely as you can.

By way of example, I would tell my story this way: I'm an abuse survivor. When I was about ten I experienced several varied encounters with sexual molestation at the hands of my father. I didn't experience penetration, nor was the abuse violent. It took place during the night, usually in my own bed. Occasionally I experienced inappropriate rubbing and fondling. Although I have no clear memory of how the abuse began, I do recall that it continued until I was eighteen years old. I didn't tell anyone for several years.

My rendering, above, is factual and to the point. But even as I write it today the power of the narrative moves me. *I survived my abuse!* Abuse shaped me, yes, but it doesn't define me. I'm an overcomer.

When you're ready, tell your own intellectual/historical story. But before you take this step, pray for courage.

2. Prayer for Courage

If you prefer not to compose a prayer in your own words, you might want to use this one: "Jesus, you know my story better than I know it myself. I ask you to protect and guard my heart as I open up, journey back in time, and tell myself the truth about my story, to the best of my ability to recall it. Strengthen me to take this important step. Relieve my fear. Grant me the will to move ahead, no longer suppressing my pain. Enable me to opt for being loosed from the haunting prison of secrecy and silence. Today I remember. I talk. I open up and tell myself the truth about my experience. With your help, Holy Spirit, I'm empowered to take this step. In Jesus' name, Amen."

◆   ◆   ◆

3. Telling Your Story at a Deeper Level

When you're honest with yourself, a significant part of your healing begins. It's as though your brain sends a message to your inner being that says; "Okay, everybody, she's opening up. We can let her know the rest of the story . . ."

I believe that this is what the following cryptic verse is all about: "Behold, You desire truth in [the] innermost being, And in the hidden part You will make me know wisdom" (Psalm 51:6, NASB). As survivors we know only too well that we have broken parts locked in secret places, expectantly yearning to be freed through the power of truth.

Of course, telling our stories isn't easy. But ignoring them, while not as jarring in the short run, isn't easy either. We exert tremendous energy in our struggles to keep our secrets under wraps. We somehow believe that if we never speak of our sexual trauma the wounds of abuse will automatically heal.

We seldom recognize that words have the power to bring life and make healing a reality. Words can bring about release and freedom. Your abuse story carries power, but without the "telling" your pain continues to swirl inside you like a funnel cloud bent on destruction.

4. Benefits of Telling

Telling yourself your story prepares you to divulge the detail to a safe, trusted ally. When you're ready to take this step, you'll find a sense of empowerment. Shame and embarrassment no longer control you.

Telling your story to someone else offers many benefits as well. It's natural to feel vulnerable, exposed, and frightened, but the more frequently you share, the more empowered you'll feel.

Everyone responds differently, but you can expect to experience

+ A sense of support, comfort, and compassion as you reveal the details.
+ Deeper intimacy with your partner.
+ Freedom from denial as you disclose the truth about what really happened to you.

+ Freedom from shame and humiliation as you break the bonds of secrecy.

+ New awareness of sexual abuse as you give others permission to shatter their own silence.

+ An end to isolation as you discover a community of fellow survivors to rally around you.

+ Important discoveries about yourself.

You're no longer running away from your past. You're looking abuse in the face and declaring, "You don't define me! God brought me through this, and He promises to use my life in amazing ways."

You refuse to allow anything else to be stolen from you.

Your time has come to live in wholeness and freedom.

GETTING TO KNOW YOURSELF

Reconnecting to the True You

I was six-years-old when he started sexually abusing me. My heart was so conflicted I simply fell asleep to cope emotionally. When I awakened from my emotional slumber, I was nineteen. Bewildered and purposeless. I've lost my childhood and I don't know the girl staring back at me in the mirror. —DELYNNE

Delynne's story was much like mine. Before I had completed elementary school, abuse had marred my identity. In my early adulthood questions rattled around in my soul.

Who am I?

Do I matter?

Why do I feel so terrible about myself?

Will I ever amount to anything?

I stumbled into maturity before I was ready—without a clue as to who I was, much less what life was supposed to be about. Worse, I didn't know where to turn to figure any of it out. This is true of many survivors. Perhaps this is the case for you or someone else you love.

For most survivors childhood was a tumultuous time. Our focus was on surviving. Our silent mantra was *Just make it through another day.* We disassociated from reality in an attempt to anesthetize ourselves from the pain. We didn't flourish like other kids. Abuse interrupted the natural unfolding of our creative, spiritual, and intellectual development. As a result, we were robbed of opportunities to experience vital *discovery stages* of life—the stages that foster a sense of worth, value, self-esteem, and confidence. We arrived at adulthood feeling like empty shells—hardened on the outside with an awareness of little or nothing on the inside. Our identity was uncultivated, splintered, and disconnected. We had grown up detached, dissociated from our true selves.

Does this sound like you? Do you wonder who you are and whether what you're doing matters? Maybe, like other survivors, you've been jogging aimlessly along on the treadmill of performance, hoping to fill your emptiness with substance and purpose. But because you haven't faced your past, your attempts at fulfillment feel futile. You believe that your contributions in life lack value.

I have a life-changing message for you: It isn't too late to know yourself and your purpose.

Your time has come. It's time to discover who you are—who God created you to be—as well as His design for *your* life of significance and fulfillment.

Along this journey you'll reconnect with the person inside you—that woman who longs to be set free from the shackles that tether you and limit your reach. You will learn how to step into a beautiful new freedom in life.

The process can't take place without work and pain, but self-discovery will be worth every step.

Roadside Check-Up

Write down three activities you enjoy. Be specific.

As you look at your list, answer the following questions:

1. Am I doing things I enjoy on a regular basis? If yes, when and in what ways do these activities fulfill me? If no, why not? What obstacles are hindering me (people, attitudes, habits, etc.)?

2. Do I enjoy doing these things even though I may not do them perfectly?

3. Do I avoid activities I might enjoy for fear of failing or because I'm

not sure where to begin? If so, examine why you suspect you're responding in this way.

4. What do the activities in which you do or do not engage reveal about yourself?

Your Personality

Physicist Jon Nelson of Ritsumeikan University in Kyoto, Japan, has researched snowflakes for fifteen years. He estimates that one cubic foot of snow can contain more than one billion snow crystals. Nelson states, "It is probably safe to say that the possible number of snow crystal shapes exceeds the estimated number of atoms in the known universe."[1] The sheer number of distinct snow crystals is amazing in itself, but more astounding still is the fact that no two of them are identical in composition.

Similarly, scientists tell us that fingerprints form from pressure on a baby's tiny, developing hands in the mother's womb. Each set of prints is unique—even identical twins do not share fingerprints.[2]

Science proves what God's Word clearly states—that you are unique. In David's inimitable words, "For you created my inmost being; you knit me together in my mother's womb. I praise you because I am fearfully and wonderfully made; your works are wonderful, I know that full well. My frame was not hidden from you when I was made in the secret place. When I was woven together in the depths of the earth, your eyes saw my unformed body. All the days ordained for me were written in your book before one of them came to be" (Psalm 139:13–16).

God formed you and breathed His life into you from the moment of your conception. He knit you together in your mother's womb and designed and engineered you to be the rare and exclusively unique woman you are today.

You're an original—not a knock-off or a copy—fashioned by the Designer par excellence, the One who gives meaning to everything beautiful in existence (which equates to everything there is!).

You're a treasure beyond compare because God has placed His stamp of authenticity, and hence of infinite, intrinsic value, on you—caring enough to fashion you, a person—in distinction from any other living being or inanimate object—in His very own image.

Better Late Than Never

Many survivors of childhood sexual abuse describe themselves as "late bloomers." At first this term may sound like a paradox. How can someone who's been prematurely exposed to sex and sexuality be a "late bloomer"? It seems more logical to think of survivors as being forced to grow up, at least in a physical sense, before their time. But in reality children of abuse are often "frozen in time."

The term "late bloomer," when applied to sexually abused children, indicates that they stop growing and developing emotionally after their first attack occurs. Recovery from child sexual abuse doesn't begin until the survivor becomes an adult . . . if it happens then. Once healing ensues, however, we can develop the strength to look deep within ourselves and make self-discoveries, some wonderful and others difficult to accept.

As a young adult I didn't identify myself as a positive person. Perhaps that aspect of my personality had been squelched, or I may have developed an "overcomer" outlook only later on in life. Either way, I'm pleased by my belated discovery that I'm a "glass-is-half-full" kind of girl. When circumstances appear to be dismal, I reframe my perspective.

I don't like injustice. I'm a fighter for the underdog, but I can become annoyed with those who settle for a "woe is me" approach to life. I prefer to motivate people to shake off the victim mindset.

These discoveries have empowered me. Knowing who I am allows me to feel fully alive and to walk out God's eternal destiny for my life.

Nature and Nurture

After years of hiding behind masks, personas, and false bravado, you know it's time to discover who you truly are and to become comfortable in your own skin. So who are you?

The oldest debate within psychology is the *Nature vs. Nurture* discussion. This dialogue centers around the question of how much of an individual's personality is shaped by these two forces:

- **Nature** refers to the unique combination of genes and hereditary that influence who we are, including (among a host of other variables) our physical appearance, intellect, abilities, health, and personality.
- **Nurture** refers to the environmental factors that influence who we are, including our early childhood experiences, family systems, social relationships, and the culture that shapes us.

Regardless of the degree to which nature or nurture has influenced your identity, these two forces have intersected to shape you. Their combined impact has resulted in your unique *character*, the composite outcome of your upbringing, cultural experiences, relationships, and genetic blueprint that represents the foundational essence of who you are.

Temperament is the balance of your personality. You inherited biologically based tendencies from each of your parents. The ways in which you're motivated, process information, and approach life were embedded in your DNA and have been part of you since those earliest days before your birth.

Since the days of ancient Greece through to the present, experts like Dr. David Keirsey, the author of *Please Understand Me*, have agreed that four different personality styles combine to create the unique core identity of each individual human. These broad, basic modes of operating are present in a distinctive mix that defines how each of us thinks, feels, and behaves.[3] Learning about these basic temperamental types will help you understand yourself.

The four basic personality types are:

1. Sanguine, *or* Influencer

Instinctive communicators, those individuals endowed with a sanguine personality serve as team cheerleaders and enthusiastic motivators, able to catch a vision and impart it to others. Theirs is the most relational of all temperaments—accepting and loving, sanguines are typically the "life" of the party. Responding well to the unexpected, they are spontaneous and agreeable.

2. Choleric, or Driver

The choleric is characterized by a dominant, direct, and decisive personality style. Such individuals are instinctive leaders who can see the big picture, accept risks, and welcome challenges with vision and optimism. The choleric can remain focused while multi-tasking, producing impressive results and obtaining desired goals, while at the same time motivating others to also produce.

3. Melancholy, or Compliant

This is the most analytical and perfectionistic temperament. The schedule-oriented melancholy personality likes to do things "correctly," work systematically, and keep every detail in view. Such individuals are self-disciplined, self-sacrificing, and loyal. Melancholy personalities are also often gifted in music, poetry, or other artistic arenas; their compliant side is introverted and reflective. They think logically, ask important questions, and work tediously until they reach consensus.

4. Phlegmatic, or Steady

Quiet and witty phlegmatics like to play it safe, preferring security and stability. They are relaxed, low-key, and easy-going. Phlegmatics are steady, kind, patient, well balanced, and comfortable keeping their emotions hidden while listening and empathizing with others' problems. They feel less comfortable when the problems or issues involve themselves personally, often resorting to an "invisible" posture until they feel it is safe to reappear.

We all possess one of these styles or, more often, a blending of two or more. Understanding these variations helps us make sense of how others may respond to situations with styles and perspectives different from our own.

In an abuse situation, for example, the choleric is the most likely to become a fighter, displaying a controlling and angry edge. Sanguine personalities, in contrast, may become excessively emotional, expressive, hot-tempered, and explosive. The phlegmatic person may express herself in a patient, methodical approach, which often comes off as dull and apathetic. Depression, suspicious thinking, and mistrust, combined with dark periods of self-reflection, would likely characterize the response of a melancholy.

You can learn more about your unique personality style by taking a "personality test" or survey. Such tools are popular and easily accessible. For your convenience, I'm providing a link (http://personality-testing.info/tests/O4TS/).

Understanding how and why you respond in relationships in the way you do will benefit you in many ways you as you move forward in your healing process.

Roadside Check-Up

1. What are some discoveries you have made about yourself in the last few years, months, or days? What new insights have you gleaned from the discussion in this chapter so far?

2. Do you consider these discoveries to be positive, negative, or neutral (merely factual or interesting)? Why? How do these facets of your personality influence your life? How, specifically, might they have influenced your response to past abuse?

3. Identify some of your likes and dislikes, as well as what you perceive to be your strengths and weaknesses.

Your Feelings

Growing up, I didn't allow myself to feel much of anything, simply because my world didn't feel safe. Most survivors can't or won't indulge in the luxury of emotions during their abusive years, and often beyond. We're convinced that feelings in and of themselves render us weak—that they're hazardous to our survival. To the contrary, we view ourselves as having to fight to survive—no one else, after all, has demonstrated an inclination to protect us.

We opt for numb because we believe numb is safer than vulnerable.

Two Extremes

Two radically different perspectives exist with regard to how people typically view or deal with their emotions. Unfortunately, either can become off balance. Frozen emotions, such as I have experienced, are representative of one extreme response, the opposite being hypersensitive emotional reactivity. At the one extreme we feel virtually nothing; at the other, we're emotively affected by practically everything. We'll explore the latter in more detail in chapter 7 in our discussion of Post-Traumatic Stress Syndrome. But it's important to understand that both extremes are defensive and manipulative responses to which survivors resort in an effort to protect their wounded soul from further hurt.

As a survivor of childhood abuse, your natural emotional development was interrupted; therefore, it wouldn't be unusual for your emotions to be underdeveloped and immature. You may live in a "both/and" reality, not just in an "either/or." You may experience periods characterized by extreme emotion and emotional outbursts, as well as seasons of feeling numb or perhaps depressed. These patterns and other aspects of emotional dysregulation may point to a more serious condition. Ask yourself whether you experience any of the following symptoms:

- ✦ Rapidly changing emotions
- ✦ Emotions that spiral out of control, leading to extreme anxiety, sadness, and rage
- ✦ Hyper-sensitive emotions that are expressed in overreactions
- ✦ Feelings of depression or despondency or suicidal thoughts
- ✦ Episodes of rage and hostility
- ✦ Overreaction to perceived slights or criticisms
- ✦ Expressing emotions in exaggerated and overly demonstrative ways

Talk through your experiences with a mental health professional, keeping in mind that extreme emotions or highly emotional behavior are not to be dismissed.

A Heart of Flesh

As you learn to identify feelings instead of stuffing them, the intensity of your emotional responses will naturally begin to dissipate. Suppressed feelings, in contrast, gain in intensity and velocity. This can be compared to the accumulated pressure of holding a beach ball underwater. The deeper you push down your emotions, the stronger they will be when they rush back to the surface, exploding out of the depths.

Emotions can make us feel vibrant and beautiful, and feelings can and do transform our world from black and white to full-blooming color. Emotions are a beautiful and mysteriously divine part of our creation as human beings formed in God's own image. The capacity to feel and to empathize sets us apart from God's other created beings and, intriguingly, makes us most like our Creator.

In the Old Testament God spoke through the prophet Ezekiel, announcing His ability to turn a cold, stony heart and into a tender, responsive entity: "I will give them an undivided heart and put a new spirit in them; I will remove from them their heart of stone and give them a heart of flesh" (Ezekiel 11:19).

Dammed-up waters can transform peaceful, meandering streams into turbulent menaces. Their roiling pressure can overtake banks and cause incredible destruction. God doesn't intend for you to live in a persistently pent-up emotional state. He created your emotions to refresh you like a bubbling, life-giving brook.

Opening ourselves up to experience emotions can be scary, however. Feelings long suppressed can easily morph into raw, intense, illogical, and even dangerous forces. Since many of us have been numb for much of our youth and young adulthood, letting ourselves explore the world of feelings can cause trepidation, and we may wonder whether this part of the journey is really necessary.

The answer is straightforward: absolutely!

Your emotions are a big part of what makes you uniquely you. Ditto for mine. Learning about your emotions—what stirs them, how you habitually respond to them, and how you use them in relationships—is a critical component for unmasking the "hidden you."

The Feeling Guide

When I was in my twenties my repertoire of emotions was scant. I could recognize and produce eye-opening displays of anger and even rage, but I could seldom rustle up an iota of happiness or contentment. One night I was invited to sit in on a discussion group for survivors, where I was introduced to a "Feelings and Emotions Vocabulary Guide." I went home that night and posted that list on my refrigerator, where it remained for several years to help me identify what I was feeling. I've included this list of emotions for your reference as Appendix 4 in the back of the book.

Roadside Check-up

Psychologists suggest the following process to help you explore and discover what you're *feeling*.

1. Identify how you feel.

Sit quietly and close your eyes. Ask yourself, *What am I feeling?* Wait and pay attention to your thoughts and feelings. It's fine if nothing surfaces, but be careful not to squelch emotions and sensations that do rise to the surface.

2. Discern the source of your feelings.

Evaluate the moments that led to your feelings. They're knocking at your heart for some reason. Did someone hurt you or criticize you? Are you nervous about an upcoming event or holiday? Have you been rejected or overlooked? Did you offend someone else? Do you need to have a conversation with a loved one to clear the air? Embrace whatever comes to you without analyzing, judging, or excusing the feelings. There's no shame in simply exploring emotions.

3. Acknowledge your feelings.

It's okay to feel uncomfortable. Stay open and vulnerable as you reflect. Be honest and acknowledge that this feeling (or combination of feelings)— whether you think it's right or wrong—is yours. Remember that emotions in themselves are neutral; there's no shame in any feeling.

Allow yourself to feel hurt, sad, angry, embarrassed, afraid, or any other emotion without condemning yourself or heaping shame on yourself by labeling the emotions as silly, stupid, irrational, or any other pejorative or demeaning term. Your feelings belong to you, and it's okay for you to experience any or all of them and to process them in a healthy way.

4. Release and express your feelings.

Feelings and emotions usually dissipate when we give them voice. Psychotherapist Kali Munro offers the following wisdom in her online article "What to Do with Your Feelings":

+ Focus on how you feel. Open your mouth and let a sound emerge from that feeling.
+ Move with the feeling. You can dance, stomp around, kick . . .
+ Scream. If you're worried about the sound, you can scream into a pillow.
+ Cry. If you feel like crying, give yourself permission to do so.
+ Write or draw from within this feeling place. Don't censor yourself; instead, let the feeling do the writing or drawing.
+ Express out loud what you feel the need to say to someone else.
+ Tell someone supportive how you're feeling.[4]

5. Comfort and reground yourself.

Speak softly and kindly to yourself, reminding yourself that you're in a safe and loving environment and that you're going to be fine. Take a few deep breaths. Reassure yourself that you can handle the emotions, reminding yourself in particular that God is with you, helping you on this journey and allowing you to borrow from his inexhaustible store of strength.

◆　◆　◆

Your Body

As a result of sexual abuse trauma, we survivors often see our bodies through a distorted lens. Sometimes we don't even *see* our body—we block out that image altogether from our mind's eye.

After abuse I lived with a love-hate relationship with my body. I wasn't sure whether it was my friend or my enemy. I became so body-conscious that I walked with slumped, rounded shoulders, trying to conceal myself from onlookers or from being "undressed by the eyes of men." My mother's voice still rings in my ears, gently instructing me, "Stand up straight, honey; you're slouching." I was awkward, pigeon-toed, and uncoordinated. My family often lamented, "Dawn is our clumsy one." To make matters worse, I was as pale as milk and freckled from head to toe, and I couldn't seem to find a reason not to dislike myself.

Healing teaches us how to find and maintain a healthy relationship with our bodies. God has given us our bodies as a gift, but we too easily despise and reject his good gift to us because someone else has abused it. Why, given these circumstances, would we think of it as valuable?

Perhaps you can relate.

Roadside Check-up

1. How do you feel about the various parts of your body?

2. What aspects do you like? What aspects do you dislike?

3. In what ways are you rejecting your body? How do you think this behavior may be linked to your abuse?

Your Body

So why do you think we battle negative feelings about our bodies? Here are some thoughts:

Your body has betrayed you.
Many survivors feel as though their bodies have betrayed them. Your body was physically manipulated, and it responded (whether or not you willed it to) to sexual touch. It's a simple fact of biology—bodies are made to respond to sexual stimuli. But often survivors experience deep shame because they believe a pleasurable physical response means they that they wanted and/or enjoyed the experience. Satan stirs this lie into the cauldron of our emotions. But you don't have to believe it and disown your body. Instead of rejecting your body, you can actively choose to celebrate it. Your body, after all, worked just the way it was designed to work. God engineered the human body with intricate precision, and your biology didn't fail. Affirm yourself for having a healthy body that responded in the God-intended way.

Your body is awkward.
You don't trust your body to perform well. You doubt you'll be graceful or strong or coordinated enough to do so. Maybe your family told you that you're clumsy. Or you've been labeled unfeminine—you know, the "athletic type." Feeling body conscious isn't uncommon for women who've been sexually assaulted. When continuous attention is directed toward our bodies, it's common for us to feel insecure, fearful, or angry.

Your body feels exposed.
You've experienced forced exposure. You were naked—both physically and emotionally. Now you most likely don't want to deal with body issues at

all, so you cover your body and try to disconnect from it in any way you can. Wrapping it up in bulky, unattractive layers of clothing is one way to conceal your body. Gaining weight is another way to "arm" yourself against potential perpetrators. You may subconsciously reason, *If I'm invisible and no one can see me, they won't be able to hurt me. I'm safe when I'm covered. No one will bother me if I'm fat.*

Your body feels unattractive.
Survivors feel soiled, dirty, and flawed. They believe that their body is "bad." Sexual abuse stole your sense of value and worth, so now when you look in the mirror, instead of seeing your worthiness you associate your image with disgrace, perhaps even seeing a disgusting wretch deserving shame. Many women admit that no matter what they do to alter their appearance— make-up, hairstyles, plastic surgeries, exercise, or weight loss—they still feel ugly. This inability to perceive or accept beauty and worth is a direct result of the psychological distortion and consequent self-rejection the sexual assault has produced.

◆　◆　◆

Now that you've embarked on your healing journey, it's time for you to get in touch with your body—and while you're at it to gain a glimpse of how wonderful and special your body is, as well as of its true purpose. In an earthly, human sense it may be said that your body belongs to you. It follows that, now that you're a consenting adult, barring unforeseen extenuating circumstances it's up to you to choose with whom you will share it and how it will be used.

God's revelation will change your view of your body when you honestly confront the truth.

A New Revelation

After the births of my babies and as I transitioned into my thirties, my body and fat cells became close, dear friends. In fact, they developed a covenant relationship, reminding me of the one between the biblical Naomi and her daughter-in-law Ruth. You know the drill: "Where you go I will go; where you stay, I will stay. Your people will be my people and your God my God. Where you die, I will die and there I will be buried. May the LORD deal with me, be it ever so severely, if even death separates you and me" (Ruth 1:16–17). You get the idea.

Then one day I encountered a rhetorical question from the apostle Paul: "Don't you know that your bodies are temples of the Holy Spirit, who is in you, whom you have received from God? You *are not your own*; you were bought at a price. Therefore honor God with your bodies" (1 Corinthians 6:19–20, emphasis mine). Suddenly the revelation hit me: *Wow! God owns my body. He bought me with a price. Jesus paid not only for my spirit and soul— my mind, will, and emotions—but for my body as well.*

At first I wasn't sure how I felt about this novel concept of Jesus' buying, and thus owning, my body. The thought of "being owned" triggered uncomfortable feelings for me. But then I remembered another story from the Bible, this one from the Old Testament, about how God redeemed a woman named Gomer (if you're a little older, and thus have a slightly longer history with television sitcoms, try to disassociate the narrative from any unbidden image your mind may conjure up of the inimitable Gomer Pyle!).

Gomer had struggled with sexual sin. The story doesn't let us in on what may have happened in her past but only that she had for whatever reason become a prostitute. She was used and abused and reused by men . . . until God instructed his faithful prophet Hosea to rescue (as in marry!) her. God used the unfortunate Hosea to illustrate His unconditional love toward an adulterous people who continually lusted—and ran—after other lovers. Hosea dutifully took Gomer home and loved her, but she ran away from him, rejected God, and willfully returned to her accustomed life of brokenness and bondage.

But God wasn't finished with Gomer. He sent Hosea to seek her out in a grimy slave market, destitute and no doubt despairing of life itself as she stood on the auction block like a chunk of beef on the hoof. Incredibly, Hosea redeemed her (bought her back) from slavery for fifteen shekels of silver and thirteen bushels of barley (Hosea 3:2). Hosea's love for Gomer was so profound that he re-rescued the prostitute he'd rescued in the first place, the one who'd run away from him back to a voluntary life of bondage. The story may not be well known, but the picture—and what is represents in terms of our own redemption—is unforgettable. In a strikingly similar manner Jesus *bought us* (as in each one of us; the picture isn't just corporate) to protect, cleanse, and rescue us from the bonds of slavery.

God owns your body, which makes you the *steward*, guardian, or trustee of your physical body, not its owner. In case you're scratching your head over this one, the definition of *steward* is "a person who manages another's property or financial affairs; one who administers anything as the agent of another or others." "Steward" is simply an old-fashioned word for "manager."

I've pondered what it means to be a good manager over something that doesn't belong to me. Being faithful, honest, and trustworthy over someone else's property is certainly a part of being a good manager. But what does it mean to be a *faithful* manager over *people*? To raise the stakes still further, not just any people but the people who exclusively and uniquely belong to God?

I suppose, at the very least, that a faithful steward over God's people should be patient, loving, kind, supportive, and empowering and should motivate, promote their personal growth, and encourage them to stretch and push themselves to do their very best.

So shouldn't I steward *my* body, which serves *me*, in the same way? The thought hit me like lightning.

My body is the living part of me that houses my spirit and soul—the living "vehicle" God has given me to *serve me as I serve Him.* He owns it, but I'm its manager. Shouldn't I speak to, refer to, and treat my body in the same way I would someone else who might be working under and serving me?

If I addressed my staff or fellow church members in the tone of voice and vocabulary I too often use to speak to, or about, my body, they'd up and quit! Why? Because no one can thrive in an environment of disrespect.

I understand people's intrinsic value; therefore, I speak gently and with kindness to those who serve me. I intentionally show appreciation and thank and praise my coworkers frequently for their efforts. And I try to perceive when individuals are in need of some extra attention or rest.

Your body and mine are gifts from God. He owns them, but we're entrusted with their stewardship. This truth has gigantic implications in terms of what we eat, how we treat our body, how we maintain and exercise it, how we present or display it, and many other aspects of our physical life. It was liberating for me to grasp the truth that my body serves me, carrying my spirit and soul while I live on this earth and thereby enabling me to accomplish my God-given purpose here.

To that I can only say "Good job, body!"

"Good job, lungs; you're breathing well."

"Good job, legs; you're strong and steady."

"Good job eyes; you're still focusing."

"Good job, heart, liver, and digestion system. Good job, body!"

God instructs us at various points in His Word to speak blessings and not curses. So why pinch the extra skin around your middle and mutter words about a muffin top? Why grumble about cellulite, wrinkles, jowls, double chins, dark spots, or dark circles? Instead, bear in mind that your intricately and lovingly designed body is working 24/7 for you—and thus ultimately for the Maker you represent. So reach your arms around yourself (at least as far as they'll go), give yourself a hug, and encourage, "Good job, beautiful, wonderful body. We're in this race together, and you're doing a fabulous job. Thank you!"

Since God owns your body, your sexual abuse wasn't committed against you alone. The abuse was committed against *God's body*. He calls on you to step back and allow Him to administer the vengeance. The *when and how* of His retribution are up to Him, but you can feel loved, valued, and vindicated, knowing that God promises to rise up as a champion on your behalf.

Roadside Check-up

Take a moment to become aware of your body. Tense and then release its various areas, moving from your forehead down through to your neck, shoulders, torso, abdomen, and buttocks. Flex and then relax your arms and hands, moving on to your thighs and down your legs through to your calves, ankles, feet, and toes.

As you do so, mouth this prayer: "Lord, thank you for my body. I praise you for giving me such a wonderful gift. Now I give it back to you. You're the owner and I'm the steward. I will take good care of this body. I will bless and not curse the frame you've seen fit to give me. I receive my body—my shape and size, my weight and height, my color and gender, all as a gift from you. Today I look into the mirror and accept ME, just as you have made me, and I say with gratitude, 'Good job, body!'"

Your Voice

As a survivor of childhood sexual trauma, you may hear a cacophony of competing voices in your head. Shaming voices, fearful voices, demeaning and cruel voices are usually all a part of the internal dialogue that takes place continuously and unrelentingly in our minds, both day and night.

The time has come for you to recognize your own, true voice. You may find yourself asking questions like *What are my thoughts? Opinions? Ideas? Do they matter?*

The answer is an unequivocal *Yes!* Your ideas DO matter. Especially to God.

One survivor said to me, "I don't have the guts to determine my own opinion. I'm too scared." Another expressed, "I don't have a clue what I think or what I like or what I want to do. I can't make a decision to save my life." Many survivors not only question the trustworthiness of their own voice but subconsciously question their right to so much as *have a voice.*

If that sounds like you, let me be the first to assure you that you have a God-given voice, along with a responsibility to share your voice in healthy ways. If you haven't been in touch with your true voice—that authentic inner voice that tells you "I can have an opinion that contributes in meaningful ways"—I encourage you to listen for the cry of your heart that's longing to be unleashed. As you learn to recognize and listen to your voice, you'll find empowerment to make decisions and regain appropriate control over your life—rightful control that was stolen by abuse.

Finding Your Authentic Voice

I use the word "authentic" because I recognize that imbalance occurs among survivors. Survivors who are angry and feel the need to spew negative comments and rage at every opportunity often resort to a false voice as a cover. They aren't using their voice as God intended when they give in to rash or venomous outbursts.

Verbal spewing is hardly a sign of health and wholeness. Overly opinionated, demanding, and demeaning remarks reveal that we are survivors still en route to healing.

◆　◆　◆

Your voice counts, and your ideas, underdeveloped and unexplored though they may be, have purpose and value. As you become whole you will want to develop your voice. The following steps will help you identify opinions, ideas, and thoughts that are authentic and true to you:

+ Be aware of issues surrounding you. Fight the urge to dissociate.
+ Start a conversation with yourself about a topic and conduct your own mental debate.
+ Educate yourself about issues.
+ Be willing to listen to others' opinions—both pros and cons.
+ Discover what experts and Christian leaders have to say on the subject at hand.
+ Find out what God has to say about the issue.
+ Ask yourself if what you hear from others is reasonable and logical.
+ Decide what *you* believe. Be willing to state it and stand by it.
+ Keep an open mind as you grow in your belief and understanding.

Roadside Check-up

+ Learn to *recognize* and *listen to* your voice.
+ Differentiate your thoughts and ideas from the traffic noise in your

head and heart. Ask yourself questions like *What do I hear? What do I feel?* and *What do I need?*

- Start a conversation with God, beginning with an open-ended "Lord, here I am."
- Sit quietly and listen for a response.

Frequently the Holy Spirit will speak in a whisper. He wants to commune with the truest part of you—that part that's beyond—and impervious to—the noise, the anger, and the masks. God wants to dialogue with *you*.

◆ ◆ ◆

You will need time—and practice—to learn to trust your voice. But as you continue to listen to your heart, refusing to reject or dismiss what you think and feel, you'll become more comfortable trusting yourself. Your confidence and self-esteem will blossom. Be assured that God will restore your true voice to you.

Your Boundaries

In their book titled *Boundaries: When to Say Yes, How to Say No to Take Control of Your Life*, doctors Henry Cloud and John Townsend have this to say: "Boundaries define us. They define *what is me* and *what is not me*. A boundary shows me where I end and someone else begins, leading me to a sense of ownership."[5]

We create personal boundaries to formulate reasonable, safe, and permissible guidelines by which we expect people to behave around us and toward us. Boundaries help us determine how to respond when someone steps beyond those limits.

I had no idea know what boundaries were, and I certainly didn't realize that I was allowed to have them or that young people were encouraged to establish them as a part of learning to become responsible adults. I was baffled at the notions of personal space and of self-respect. I didn't recognize that I had both a choice and a voice regarding who could touch me and the kinds of treatment I wasn't obligated to tolerate. Even after learning what boundaries were, I lacked the courage to identify and enforce my own. Today I like to think of boundaries as safety fences. They identify my personal limits, while allowing me to interact with others in healthy and enjoyable ways. As an old adage would have it, "Good fences make good neighbors." Healthy boundaries allow us the freedom and direction to tear down our carefully constructed fortress walls of self-protection and learn instead to construct permeable, life-giving fences allowing input to flow freely, safely, and unimpeded in both directions.

Women who've experienced sexual trauma are often naïve or timid about placing boundaries. Reasons for this hesitancy may include

+ Feeling that we lack any rights.
+ Fear that setting boundaries will jeopardize our relationships.
+ Feeling awkward with boundaries because we have never learned to set or maintain them.
+ Ignoring our own needs in favor of meeting the needs of others.
+ Lack of confidence and not knowing how to define our likes and dislikes.
+ Struggles with distorted thinking.
+ Ignorance of what healthy boundaries look like.

Those of us who've been abused probably grew up unaware that we possessed any rights. After all, our assailants hadn't respected our personal space. We'd been violated and stripped of our voices, leaving us feeling defeated, worthless, and powerless.

From time to time I enjoy a massage. My masseuse works on the knots and kinks in my back and neck, and the feeling is awesome! But often the masseuse finds a knot and presses on it with all her strength—bringing me to tears with the stinging pain.

My tendency is to stoically absorb the pain in silence. Even when she asks "How's the pressure?" I continue to "grin and bear it." I lost my voice, after all, when I was ten years old. The fact is that I'm still working on how to speak up for myself—even when I'm in pain.

Like me, you have God-given rights. You have the right to say no or yes. You have the right to be treated with love and respect. You may wince and pronounce "Ouch, that hurts!" or you may exhale and sigh "Yes, I like that." You may assert your right either to indulge in a nap or to work overtime. You may, and indeed must, require people you hire to follow the guidelines of your workplace, and you owe it to yourself and others to voice your need for food or sleep or privacy or company. You have the right to feel and appropriately express your emotions. You have the prerogative to change your mind and the obligation to keep your commitments. God has given you freedom, and you may choose how you want to use it.

But God's ultimate desire is that none of us uses our freedom to transgress others' God-given rights. That's abuse. We should know: we may be in the process of healing, but to some extent abuse has forever changed us.

It's up to us to break the cycle, to create and enforce reasonable, safe, and healthy boundaries, both for ourselves and for those we love.

Roadside Check-Up

Take a moment to think about your personal boundaries.

1. Have you set healthy boundaries for yourself? If not, why not?

2. How well do you enforce personal boundaries?

3. Make a list of the boundaries you'd like to incorporate and feel God is leading you to implement.

4. Why do you believe these boundaries should be priorities?

5. What often prevents you from implementing boundaries? What do you believe could become an obstacle to your success in implementing the above boundaries?

Setting boundaries can mean disappointing someone else by saying no. Since many survivors are people pleasers, saying no to someone we love can be painfully difficult. We fear a loss of relationship if we don't do exactly what others want us to. Implementing boundaries means exerting firmness, applying self-discipline, and identifying our likes and dislikes—all skills that don't come easily for survivors. However, as we learn to practice healthy boundaries we find that we also learn to instruct others about what behaviors are acceptable toward us. Implementing boundaries teaches us how to respect both others and ourselves.

However, setting boundaries is only one side of the equation; the other side is consequences. In order for a boundary to be effective we have to do more than just define and announce it—we have to defend and enforce it. If we don't attach consequences for infractions of the boundary, it isn't a boundary at all but only a threat. A true boundary consists of at least two components. For example: "If you ever hit me again [part 1], I'll call the police [part 2]." The first part establishes the line in the sand: "*If you . . . ,*" while the second stipulates what it is you promise to do if the individual makes the decision to cross that line: "*I will . . . .*" Make sure that you are prepared and able, both mentally and physically, to carry out the consequences you attach to your boundary.

We must grasp the purpose of setting boundaries in order to fully appreciate the importance of implementing them. Drawing lines and setting limits aren't meant to be selfish and mean-spirited. Nor are boundaries intended to punish, manipulate, or control others in order to get our way. We set boundaries for the purpose of our own protection, health, and well-being, enabling us to thrive.

For more information on this critical issue see Appendix 5, "Understanding Your Personal Boundaries."

Your Purpose

I don't know what potential I might have fulfilled if I hadn't been sexually abused.

I often think about my lost opportunities. I wonder in what ways I might have excelled had I not been compelled to cope with the secrets of my trauma.

What might I have achieved?

What might I have accomplished if emotional paralysis hadn't crippled me?

Maybe you've had similar thoughts. But the truth is that it's never too late to discover and reclaim your unique calling and purpose. Sexual abuse may have stolen your past, but it can't rob you of your future once you decide to rise up and grasp the hope and healing available to you.

I hope you'll join me in asserting, "We are *not what has happened to us*; we are daughters of God, with a special future and a promise from Him. The promise of Jeremiah 29:11 may have been specific to God's Old Testament people, but the prophet's words still speak to us in terms of what we know of our Creator Father's character and intentions for those He loves (that means *us!*): "'I know the plans I have for you,' declares the LORD, 'plans to prosper you and not to harm you, plans to give you hope and a future.'" Listen as well to these lesser known words of encouragement from another Old Testament prophet: "The LORD your God is with you, the Mighty Warrior who saves. He will take great delight in you; in his love he will no longer rebuke you, but will rejoice over you with singing" (Zephaniah 3:17). Why not pause for a moment and allow the implications to sink in?

Begin with a Name Change

Getting to know your purpose begins with a name change. Why? Because your label—indicative as it is of your identity—makes a difference.

I alluded earlier to the lovely short story encapsulated in the Old Testament book of Ruth. We read there about a woman named Naomi, a woman whose name means "my joy." Every time someone called out to her, they were in effect exclaiming, "Hello, my Joy!"[6]

A severe famine struck Naomi's home country, so together with her husband, Elimelech, and their two young sons Naomi emigrated to a neighboring country called Moab. While the family was living in this foreign land, the boys grew up and married. Soon, however, tragedy struck—not once but three times in succession. Naomi's husband died, followed soon after by the deaths of both her sons in a battle. With the famine now over a desolate Naomi decided to move back to her hometown. Upon her arrival her old friends greeted her in their accustomed manner: "Hello, Naomi. Long time, no see."

But Naomi reprimanded them, directing them no longer to call her Naomi but to substitute the name Mara, meaning "bitter sorrow." The old identity no longer fit.

Why insert this seemingly unrelated account at this point? Because we often do the same thing as Naomi: we allow circumstances to interrupt our life's course and alter our identity—in effect, to change our name. We let experiences define who we are and determine our essence, not to mention our purpose and future prospects.

You've experienced a horrific blow to your self-worth and identity: sexual abuse has punctured the very core of your soul, and the trauma has reshaped you and re-labeled you. The truth is that *this*—the onset of your healing process—is precisely the *right* time for you to change your name. It isn't Victim, Shame, Ruined, or Ugly. Nor is it Mara! You're Beautiful. Your name is Joy. Freedom. Glorious Future. These names capture your essence.

And your name change places you on the exciting threshold of discovering your purpose.

◆　　◆　　◆

From Pauper to Purpose

In his book *The Purpose Driven Life* author Rick Warren states, "Long before you were conceived by your parents, you were conceived in the mind of God. He thought of you first."

In other words, you aren't a mistake, a mess-up, or a fluke. You aren't here accidentally. You're the intentional design of God Almighty. It's His desire (has been His desire, in fact, since before the beginning of time) for *you* to be vitally alive—now, on this earth, at this precise moment in time. You aren't the result of happenstance; God created you with the exact precision with which He accomplishes all His work—just the way He wants you, to fit the exclusive purpose and plan He's had in mind for you from before time began. That means that your physical, emotional, and intellectual blueprint were sketched out in the heart of God eons before you drew a single breath.

The psalmist David states this truth in unforgettable terms: "For you created my inmost being; you knit me together in my mother's womb. I praise you because I am fearfully and wonderfully made; your works are wonderful, I know that full well. My frame was not hidden from you when I was made in the secret place. When I was woven together in the depths of the earth, your eyes saw my unformed body. All the days ordained for me were written in your book before one of them came to be" (Psalm 139:13–16).

As God impeccably formed each of us He lovingly implanted within our psyches the seeds of our potential and destiny. In just the right environment and culture, and at just the right time and place, these seeds were meant to thrust their way to the surface of our lives, to bloom and produce beautiful and bountiful fruit. We sense the presence of these seeds deep inside us, as our chests pound with desire when ideas and dreams bubble up in our souls. Each of us was created to fulfill a unique purpose, and sexual abuse has no power to rob us of our destiny!

Since God planted within us the seeds of promise, it makes sense that to understand our purpose we must begin by looking to our Master Designer. Rick Warren's book *The Purpose Driven Life* guides us in this discovery. I include his chapter headings here as a catalyst to guide your reflection. As he reveals,

You were planned for God's pleasure.
A fulfilling relationship with God is intrinsic to your purpose.

You were formed for God's family.
You were created to belong to and function within a family of other people, all of whom are living out their purposes, too.

You were created to become like Christ.
Your purpose includes having a character patterned after Jesus'. This character is developed through the shaping, building, and transforming function of the Holy Spirit, who works in and through life's varied experiences, including its trials.

You were shaped for serving God.
You're on this earth to change the world through serving with your unique gifts and talents.

You were made for a mission.
God wants to use your life to reveal Himself to others.

You have an amazing future in God. The moment has come for you to take captive the lies that have taken up residence in your mind and heart, to throw them out the door and invite your rightful life of promise to fill the vacancy.

Roadside Check-up

Choose a quiet place. Clear your mind from distractions and ask God for His loving presence to envelop you. Listen for His "still, small voice" within you (check out 1 Kings 19:12 in the KJV for the context of this well-known, if archaic, terminology). Don't overthink or argue with yourself. Answer each question with your first, instinctive response and write down your answers:

1. What is it that makes me smile all the way to my soul?

2. What am I doing when I feel most fully alive?

3. What activity makes me lose track of time?

4. What activities make me feel good about myself? Great?

5. What things inspire me and infuse in me a sense of wonder?

6. What skills, abilities, or talents come naturally for me?

7. In what ways do I feel called to use the talents, passions, and values I've been given for the purpose of serving others?

8. The loss of my ability to participate in which activity would make me sad?

9. If I had to give a message to a large group of people, who would those people be? What would my message be?

10. What makes me feel closest to God?

When we discover the passions that kindle a fire in our soul and instill a smile in our hearts, we gain insight into our God-given purpose.

Don't limit God; His boundless love defines you beyond the false boundaries of abuse.

You're a survivor.

You're courageous.

And the greatest truth of all: God adores you and has incomprehensible, eternity-altering plans for your life.

FACING THE REALITY MIRROR
Honoring Yourself by Acknowledging Your Pain

*I do not believe that sheer suffering teaches. If suffering alone taught,
all the world would be wise, since everyone suffers. To suffering must
be added mourning, understanding, patience, love, openness, and a
willingness to remain vulnerable.* —ANNE MORROW LINDBERGH

Vulnerable

I was terrified to recognize and admit that horrifying things had been done
to me and that the unspeakable wrong known as *sexual abuse* had left me
susceptible and wounded. I felt overwhelmed by the systematic injuries
done to my body, mind, and soul. In fact, I refused to face the scars of sexual abuse and to honestly look at how my father had marred my spirit or
to acknowledge the enormity of what he had stolen from me. The thoughts
were simply too painful. So I hid from the truth about my life and constructed an alternate paradigm of reality that I promised myself would protect me from facing how hurt I really was.

I didn't know how wrong I was.

Following are classic self-protective strategies of thinking adopted by
abuse survivors, including me:

Denial

I minimized my trauma. And once my abuse stopped I denied that I was
experiencing "complications" from its aftermath.

*Others may struggle, but not me. What happened didn't really affect me
that much.*

After I had renewed my commitment to Christ and resumed attending church, I convinced myself that if I were only to forgive my father all my pain would disappear. So I vehemently refused help, declaring to myself and to others, "I've forgiven him. I'm not rehearsing the past. It's over and I'm fine."

But it wasn't over and I most certainly wasn't fine.

I'm not sure whether to laugh or cry when I think in retrospect about my attitude. I was wrong on every account. To begin with, I had in no way actually forgiven my father. Second, my trauma wasn't over; and third, I wasn't even remotely fine. Like millions of other survivors, I eventually learned the hard truth that *the pain of abuse isn't over when it's over!*

I was living in denial (or, as I prefer to call it, a state of selective amnesia). I didn't *want to* remember. I was trying to ignore the reality of my sexual abuse, but my attempts were tantamount to trying to ignore overwhelming destruction in the aftermath of a hurricane.

Emotional debris littered my life. My wounded soul lay unresponsive in the rubble. I kept trying to pull myself back up to my feet, but every time I tried I fell backward, exhausted and defeated. I couldn't effect my own healing, and I couldn't accept any offer of help until I was ready to look at myself in the mirror and acknowledge, "Dawn, you're hurting. You're angry. And you aren't living. You're existing."

We can't be freed from our pain until we first acknowledge that we're in pain and need to be healed. And that we want to know our true selves—the woman God created each of us to be.

When I looked in the mirror I didn't know the strange girl gazing forlornly, with those vacant eyes, back at me. What was more frightening was that I wasn't sure I wanted to know her. Instead, I felt angry and disgusted at this imposter inhabiting my body.

I hated myself.

And what was worse, I didn't know how to eradicate those feelings.

Self-Contempt

I had to face the reality of my self-loathing.

If I were going to jumpstart my arrested development, grow, and heal,

I had to stop rejecting the stranger in the mirror. The time had come for me to confront my self-contempt and honor myself by acknowledging my pain, discovering how it had shaped me, and learning who it was God had created me to be.

How about you? Do you affirm yourself? Do you honor and validate the little girl inside you? Have you let her speak to the adult you and tell her story? She was wounded, hurt, confused, and abandoned, and her pain is worthy of your compassion, curiosity, and care. You've admitted that your sexual abuse did in fact occur, and you're growing increasingly aware of those elusive details of your story. The time has come to take the next step: risk vulnerability. Admit the injury sexual trauma has done to you and investigate the consequences and effects.

Inventory what has been stolen from you. Be willing to acknowledge what you've lost and how those losses have influenced who you have become.

Refuse to deny your pain or to accept contempt—from yourself or others. *You* are not what happened to you. You are not the who your abuser or abusers would have you believe you are.

When you can move beyond admitting "I've been sexually abused" to conceding "I've been wounded and remain scarred by my sexual abuse," you'll find yourself freed to delve deeper into your emotional, psychological, and spiritual being in order to achieve more complete healing. This is yet another affirmation of your true worth and value.

As you acknowledge the magnitude of what you've endured and survived you take a powerful step forward in healing . . . and toward learning to express love for the broken, abused part of yourself. The adult, healing part of you is learning to step into your true identity as you actively participate in healing the wounds of your past.

A Fearless Inventory

When you feel ready, take an honest and thorough inventory of yourself physically, mentally, emotionally, and spiritually. Evaluate your current condition with thoughtfulness and courage, but, most importantly, allow God to illuminate truth to you during the process.

Bear in mind that this inventory has to be done *by* you *for* you. So be honest. And fearless. This approach may be new for you, so don't expect it to be easy. In the words of Lamentations 3:40, "Let us examine our ways and test them, and let us return to the LORD."

Choose when it is you're ready to start. You may want to spend some time in prayer and reflection before you begin. The purpose of the inventory is to discover how the abuse has harmed you. Although someone else may have the power to hurt you, no one else can heal you. Healing is *your work*, though it can be accomplished only with the help of the Holy Spirit and through the people and resources God provides for you.

Authentic healing cannot take place unless you **complete this process.** (I bolded these words to help you remember that healing is a *process.*) So don't expect immediate, earth-shattering results. A process is incremental and takes time. You will gain the greatest value if you don't try to rush through the steps.

Step 4 of Alcoholics Anonymous's 12-step recovery program states: "Make a searching and fearless moral inventory of ourselves."[7] Recovering addicts have ardently identified Step 4 as the *pathway to freedom.* In the Bible Jesus expresses it this way: "Then you will know the truth, and the truth will set you free" (John 8:32).

The door to freedom swings on the hinge of truth.

Since this step is so vital, let me share what a searching and fearless moral inventory might look like for a woman who has been wounded by sexual assault.

My dear friend Shellie Cole-Mickens, a psychologist, leads women through their Step 4 process. I asked her about the importance of completing a searching inventory, and she passionately gave the following "off the cuff" response. Her words are based on materials taken from the Narcotics Anonymous Manual, combined with her own experience:

> The purpose of a thorough 4th step (by the way, you'll do it numerous times as you grow emotionally, mentally, and spiritually in your recovery) is to sort through the confusion and contradictions in your life so you can find out who you "really" are. Being thorough helps you rid yourself of the burdens and traps that have controlled you and prevented your growth.

We can only be as honest with ourselves as we are aware of ourselves, and as we discover, uncover, and reveal more truth about our lives we become increasingly more discerning about ourselves and the world around us.

We are challenged to be searching, fearless, and thorough when we do a 4th step and to trust someone to help us who has a "working" knowledge of the steps and who understands that we are experts at self-deception. Completing this process is NOT a confession of how horrible we are. As the basic text in NA suggests, most of us find that we are neither as terrible, nor as wonderful, as we have believed.

Additionally, the purpose of completing this step thoroughly is to free ourselves of living in old, useless patterns. I still find myself using antiquated survival mechanisms that have outlived their usefulness. Sometimes I hold onto the past (e.g., resentment), but a thorough inventory won't allow me to stay there. With the help of God, my sponsor, and other mentors, I'm able to free myself from myself.

Hopefully, reading Shellie's words will inspire you to begin the inventory process. On the other hand, you may feel apprehensive. The idea of delving into secret places may cause you deep anxiety.

How can I take a fearless inventory when I feel so afraid?

If this is your response, know that you aren't alone.

God will strengthen you to take the next step at your own pace. Bear in mind that this is *your* time. God knew from the infinity before creation that you'd be in precisely this place at exactly this moment. And the Holy Spirit will instill within you the courage to continue down the road of self-discovery into healing and freedom. My prayer is that you'll experience *Aha!* discoveries as you gain new insight into your fears, your dreams, your false guilt, your passions, your irritations—and every hidden nook and cranny of your soul. Be attentive to the gentle moments when Truth brushes ever so softly across your heart and blows away the shroud of deception that has for so long camouflaged the real you.

God's transformation often comes as we listen, patiently and attentively, to His quiet whispers.

Roadside Check-up

1. Take the time to pause and listen to God's nudges. Ask yourself whether the truths you've read may apply to you. Then write down your responses (in short form in the space provided or in greater detail, perhaps in a journal). Try to keep your mind open and to avoid dismissing what you may have passed off or passed over as non-issues for your life. Be aware of your defense mechanisms, and pray for sensitivity and the power of the Holy Spirit to help you lay aside defensiveness, self-protectiveness, anger, repression, minimizing, and other past coping mechanisms.

2. In what ways have I acknowledged the pain done to me?

3. How have I been injured?

4. How have my wounds changed me?

5. What do I grieve?

6. How have I suffered in the aftermath of the sexual abuse in my past?

7. Do I believe that God can and will heal me?

8. Do I believe that He can and will heal the little girl inside me?

◆ ◆ ◆

"Dropped" But Not Forgotten

After I had completed my fearless inventory, I cried.

And cried.

And cried some more.

Up until that time I hadn't released tears for myself. I hadn't allowed myself to grieve for the frightened little girl inside me and for her lost childhood. I hadn't allowed myself to look seriously at my pain and to admit that someone who should have loved me had, instead, hurt me so badly. Instead, I'd done all I could to deny release to the torrent of tears I was holding inside.

Then one day I heard the story of a young child who, like me, had been painfully "dropped" by the circumstances of life.

I heard the story of Mephibosheth.

Mephibosheth was the son of Prince Jonathan and the grandson of King Saul.

When Mephibosheth (from hereon called Phib) was five years old, the gruesome battle of Mount Gilboa broke out, and both his father, Jonathan, and his grandfather, King Saul, were killed.

Upon hearing of the tragedy, Phib's nursemaid feared for the safety of her young charge and fled with him to the royal residence. She knew that the leader of a new royal dynasty would likely execute every potential heir of the former dynasty, and Phib was in mortal danger. But in her haste in fleeing she dropped Phib, and both of his feet were maimed in the fall. From that day forward he was crippled, unable to walk. In those days a lame man was considered useless—unable to work and, therefore he was dependent upon the charity of others for the remainder of his life—a truly hopeless position. Phib was not only a fugitive but also a disabled man totally dependent upon others to provide for his every need.

From Gibeah, Phib was carried to the land of Gilead, where he and his nurse found refuge for many years in the house of Machir at Lo-Debar. According to Biblehub.com, the name *Lo Debar* means a place without pasture and thus without hope—a place of total desolation. Imagine the most "God-forsaken" locale you've ever seen. What would it be like to live in that environment? To be exiled to survive as an outcast in a place of hopelessness? There at Lo Debar, Phib was left to live out the rest of his days undercover. Paralyzed and isolated, he vegged in a place where no one would be likely to care enough to search him out.

And for a while, no one did.

Like Phib, you, my friend, were "dropped" by the circumstances of life. Someone you love may have tried to keep you safe, but they failed, and you became the victim of a heinous crime—or a protracted and seemingly unending series of them! Your abuse maimed you in body, soul, and spirit. Afterward you were carried to a place where your secret would be kept under wraps, but your soul was abandoned. Lo Debar: a place of *not having*, a place of no hope, of emotional desolation. Swept away from your former life of promise, you were forsaken to live out the remainder of your days, broken by silence and huddled, hiding, in desolation and desperation.

You have lived your life since that time believing that no one would ever know what had really happened to you, let alone care.

Does this situation describe the ending you envision for your story?

It doesn't have to be that way if you'll only acknowledge your wounds and stop living a broken life.

It doesn't have to be that way if you'll only stop denying the aftermath of your abuse and continuing to huddle there in the shadows.

It doesn't have to be that way if you'll only give the broken, abused child inside you a voice; listen to her; patiently allow her to blurt out, at her own pace and in her own vocabulary, her pain and losses and grief; comfort her; and allow her to live out a full life of renewed purpose.

Phib's story ends happily. God provided an ending, in fact, far more amazing than anything Phib could ever have dreamed possible. Many years after his arrival in Lo Debar, a compassionate and generous King David—a man after God's own heart—went to the trouble of searching for Phib and found him living in desolation and disability. The king rescued the son of his deceased soul mate, Jonathan, and brought him home to the royal palace, where once again Phib sat, entitled, at the king's table, recognized as royalty instead of ridiculed as a pauper. For the rest of his life Phib enjoyed the benefits of membership in the king's royal family.

Right now, you too are being summoned: come on out of LoDebar. You no longer have to live in desolation.

God is prepared to set you in a place of honor. Begin by honoring yourself by speaking these words: "Today I will take my first steps as I will walk into my true identity!"

Roadside Check-up

1. How have you responded to your abuse in the past?

2. What behaviors or coping skills were useful to you as a child or in the past but no longer serve you well?

3. Are those limited coping skills doing you more harm than good, effecting more damage than healing? In what ways?

4. Of what are you afraid, and how do those fears prevent you from living in freedom and fullness?

ENDING THE SHAME GAME
Shedding Your Secrets and Shame

I am invisible. This should make me happy because I want to hide. I want the eyes of all to look away from me, for I am unworthy of any notice. Yet, on the rare occasion when I am seen, I feel the rush of hope; hope that I could be loved. That's when shame reminds me 'love is not for you.' I blush in my soul and I want to hide. I am invisible. —A SURVIVOR

The Realities of Shame

Shame.

Over the years abuse has woven the emotions, weight, and bondage of shame into our identities, to the point that it has seemingly become an intrinsic part of the warp and weft of who we are.

Painful feelings of humiliation have birthed in us a profound sense of degradation and unworthiness.

Shame may be described as a combination of strong feelings that include degradation, disgrace, dishonor, embarrassment, inadequacy, and/or profound regret and self-disappointment. The word's original meaning is "to cover."[8] Shame compels us into the shadows, where we cower and attempt to cover ourselves. It imbues us with an intense and often illogical fear of exposure, which debilitates us and steals our potential.

Shame works like Novocain, deadening us to our real emotions, our true selves, and the possibility of healthy relationships with God and others.

Perhaps you know the voice of shame. Most abuse victims are intimately acquainted with it.

Shame is typically the single greatest destructive emotion in the lives of the abuse survivors with whom I speak. They can't always express the powerful feelings that overshadow and debilitate them or predict what will trigger them, but most survivors know the death grip of shame all too well.

"When I'm in public, I feel everyone's knowing eyes looking at me. Their penetrating gaze burns right through me. They can see what I really am, and I want to run and hide from their disgust."

This survivor's shame rolls over her like a wave whenever she's in public. As a result she avoids public gatherings and chooses for the most part to remain a captive in her safe, insular home.

The renowned philosopher Jean-Paul Sartre had this to say about shame:

> In feeling ashamed we feel objectified and exposed as inherently flawed or defective before the gaze of a viewing, judging other. (Sometimes, we, ourselves, can be our viewing other.) In shame we are tyrannized and held hostage by the eyes of others; we belong, not to ourselves, but to them. In that sense, shame is indicative of an inauthentic or unowned way of existing.[9]

Eventually, the reality that shame reduces the quality of our lives to mere existence becomes obvious.

I have to avoid being found out . . . so I have to avoid others becomes the default "if/then" logical sequence. But is it accurate? Appropriate? Necessary?

Uncovering *why* we as survivors have a toxic relationship with shame is another story.

Why Shame?

Those of us who were abused as children learned at an early age that the world is anything but safe. We felt powerless and out of control. Our predictable little world had been turned upside down, and we had been forced to adapt to a distorted way of living—to distrust the supposedly trustworthy, to believe the patently false witness, and to find the only security available to us in the presence of the dangerous and unsafe. At an age that should have been marked by innocence and trust, guilt and shame took center stage, and we discovered what it felt like to *be* bad. We blamed ourselves for the disgraceful things that had happened to us because, ironically, that explanation helped us feel as though we were maintaining some semblance of control. Taking the blame helped us make sense of our sexual trauma and instilled in us a false sense of safety and security. *If the molestation was my fault, then I can stop it from happening again,* we told ourselves. That reasoning, though twisted, made us feel empowered and to some degree allayed our fear.

We held on to the emotions of guilt and shame because in some convoluted manner they also helped us protect our abuser and survive in a relationship upon which we were absolutely dependent and which we were powerless to leave. Since we probably knew our abuser—perhaps intimately so—our ability to maintain for ourselves a position of provision and protection may have demanded our silence. We learned self-talk that sounded something like *It was my fault* or *I know they love me, so it must be something I've done.* We leaned on guilt and shame and the control we believed it afforded us in order to maintain a minimal degree of functionality—even though that control was itself dysfunctional. Shame deadened the intensity of our longings. We "guilted" ourselves out of wanting anything for ourselves, squelching our natural desire for essentials like love, touch, connectivity, and affection to the point of dismissing them as unnecessary or even evil. Eventually, shame morphed into contempt. Contempt for others and ourselves deadened what might have remained of our longings and hopes. We hated ourselves for wanting and hated others for offering.

Guilt and shame falsely served *you* as a child.

Guilt continues to erode your life.

The guilt you tried to use for control now controls you.

The Shame Game

"It wasn't your fault."

No matter how many times I heard the counselor say those words, I still believed that I knew better: I was flawed and ruined.

Okay, so I'm not the person who committed a shameful act, but I AM the one left with permanent stains. I've been disgraced for life.

Survivors protect themselves. They position impenetrable shields around their hearts, constructed from contempt, secrecy, embarrassment, false pride, alienation, and self-hatred. The shield deflects life-giving words. As one survivor told me, "I can't open up my heart and risk believing in a life that's free from the shame of the past. I wouldn't be able to bear one more disappointment."

The shame-ridden soul denies access to Truth.

At the same time the wounded soul absorbs the lies, both of a false story and of a false identity: "guilty, ruined, unworthy." The abused woman believes and echoes Shame's accusing voice as she questions her culpability:

Why didn't I say no?

Why did I like how my body felt? Does that make me responsible?

What if I wore the wrong clothes?

Why didn't I scream or tell?

I loved my abuser. Does that mean I wanted it?

I felt special and accepted special gifts. Does that mean I gave my abuser permission to violate me?

They told me I wanted it—that it was my fault. What if it's true?

To the survivor who feels guilty, the seductive voice of shame sounds convincing, but its allure is deadly. Left unresolved, shame will destroy you—your future, your relationships, your freedom—in a slow, inexorable and ever-tightening stranglehold that eventually chokes the life out of you.

Incidentally, none of these or any other *whys* or *what ifs* ever make abuse your fault.

Never. Ever. Period.

So if it's not my fault, why do I blame myself? Why do I feel such deep self-loathing?

Because there's a massive disconnect between what you *know* and what you *feel* to be true, you remain powerless, at an emotional level, to escape shame's prison.

Your logical mind hears spoken affirmations of your blamelessness and wants to accept them as truth and to be set free, yet that impenetrable shield, coupled with the shame-based programming of your heart, stubbornly resists. Instead, you hold on to contempt—for people who insist on your innocence and for yourself for believing the ridiculous fantasy that you might indeed not be culpable.

When you hold contempt, you dismiss the words of your helper as foolish, and you castigate yourself for entertaining the idea of being blameless and pure.

A contemporary scholar on shame, Gershen Kaufman, puts it this way: "Shame is the most disturbing experience individuals ever have about themselves; no other emotion feels more deeply disturbing because in the moment of shame the self feels wounded from within."[10]

Roadside Check-up

1. Have you discovered that you have a toxic relationship with shame? Take a moment to read these words: "I'm not to blame. This is not my shame. I will be free from shame. Today I renounce shame and claim my innocence."

2. Read those words again—and again, until the healing power of truth begins to forge a breach in your defensive armor. What do you feel, hear, and sense as you read these words that declare your innocence? Write them down.

3. Internalize the words above. Let them settle deep within your heart—allowing your soul and spirit to believe them.

◆   ◆   ◆

Shame and Guilt

Shame is the prosecuting attorney, accusing me of a crime I did not commit, and I plead guilty. —DAWN

In my previous book, *When a Woman You Love Was Abused*, I share the difference between guilt and shame: "Guilt is when you feel like you've done something wrong. Shame is when you believe you are something wrong."

This definition captures the distinctions well. It's not the *doing* that makes us feel bad—that's guilt. It's the *being* that makes us feel despicable—that's shame.

As I've stated earlier, shame carries a deep, inner certainty of exposure. We feel naked before an accusing world. We self-loathe because we're convinced that our damaged identities have been exposed. We see ourselves as marred and imperfect and blame ourselves.

Shame says, "I'm defective, flawed, a disgrace." Shame is pervasive—a toxic soul-cancer.

When you live in shame, you alienate yourself from others and even from yourself by concealing your true identity. You reason, *I can't let anyone see who I really am because who I really am is unacceptable and bad. If I let you see who I am, you won't like me—I don't even like me.*

You hide by wearing masks and putting up false fronts, making yourself spiritually and emotionally unknown to others—and sadly, an alien to yourself.

Guilt also burdens survivors, but its effects differ from those of shame. Healthy guilt can be a positive force. Guilt helps us to distinguish right from wrong. God gifts us with a sensitive conscience that pricks us when we've committed sin. Guilt points out to us that we've violated God's law, human law, or our own personal code of ethics. Instead of driving us to bad behavior as shame does, positive guilt motivates us to make things right. Unadulterated guilt inspires us to make amends where needed, to ask for forgiveness, or to make restitution. Healthy guilt says, *I've done wrong. I know how to do better.*

Having a guilty conscience indicates that we've done something out of character, below the quality of person we believe ourselves to be. Rightly engaged, guilt demonstrates that we possess self-respect.

Misplaced guilt, however, stalks us when we take on responsibility that isn't meant to be ours or feel guilty about something that wasn't our fault—or, even, for an infringement on someone else's part.

False guilt ensnares many abuse survivors. Perhaps your perpetrator told you that his sinful behavior was *your* fault. He projected his guilt and shame on you, his victim, and you accepted it. As an innocent child you owned the guilt for participating in sexual acts you knew to be wrong, and you felt responsible. You believed that you should have or could have done something to stop your abuse.

Misplaced guilt fuels your shame, and you become trapped, to the point that you can't forgive yourself. As one woman expressed it, "I'm living out a lifetime prison sentence for a crime I didn't commit."

Survivors feel guilty about many things, among them:

+ Being abused
+ Staying silent
+ Wearing the wrong clothes
+ Feeling needy for attention
+ Being unable to stop the abuse being perpetrated on siblings
+ Feeling responsible for younger children being abused
+ Being attractive/unattractive (this one can cut both ways).

Confronting both shame and misplaced guilt is an important aspect of your recovery. When you discover the truth about your value and assign responsibility for the crime committed against you to the perpetrator, you will no longer live as a withdrawn victim, chained by the lies that have led you to view yourself as flawed, bad, and unlovable.

Kathryn and Mindy are both survivors of childhood sexual abuse. When I first met Kathryn, she was approaching a breakdown. For years she had avoided processing her childhood trauma, but when her coping strategies started failing her, she was forced to come out of hiding and deal with her abusive past. Kathryn felt herself to be out of control, and her anger had reached a boiling point, often erupting like a raging volcano. Her physical affect screamed, "Don't come near me, or I'll explode all over you."

Mindy was also nearing a breakdown. Her anger had turned inward, eroding her health and well-being like a soul-cancer. When she reached bottom she virtually collapsed—depressed, suicidal, and laden with rejection. Her affect whimpered, "Go ahead and hate me; everyone else does."

These women were suffering from the same malady. Although the symptoms manifested differently, shame hung over each of them like shingles on a rooftop. With nothing to lose, Mindy and Kathryn both started their healing journey. Today, a few years later, the three of us have become friends. While we visited over lunch recently, I was overwhelmed by the healing transformation both of these women have experienced. Kathryn's face beamed as she shared with regard to her recovery: "Shame enveloped me like a cloud. Everywhere I went, shame followed. It became my good friend; it helped me hide. When I finally broke free, I felt almost naked because its presence had been so tangible. When it left me, I was free!"

Mindy joined in with equal passion:

> Yes! That's how it was with me, too. I physically felt my shame lift after wearing it like a blanket, with me beneath peering out of a tiny hole. Then, one day Jesus told me He loved me and accepted me just as I was. I'd heard it before, but this day truth broke through. I started crying— and I never cry. Jesus told me He was setting me free from shame. The shame lifted from me like I was stepping out of an old robe. Shame had taken my life, but Jesus gave it back.

Shame is a counterfeit companion. God promises us that His presence will go with us wherever we go (Exodus 13:21–22; Nehemiah 9:19). He pledges that we will be followed by goodness and mercy all the days of our life (Psalm 23:4–6), that He will never leave us or forsake us (Hebrews 13:5b). The confirmation of God's promise to be ever-present may be found in the peace He gives to us—an all-enveloping peace that suffuses our souls. Satan's presence, on the other hand, is sensed through shame. This false friend follows us, too. Shame offers a false covering and false protection. Its promise whispers, in this case ominously, "I won't leave you or let you go."

Kathryn and Mindy each received a miracle—joy in the too-long-familiar place of shame and disgrace. This same miracle is available, for the asking, to you. Simply reach out and receive the promise of God that offers, "Instead of your shame you will receive a double portion, and instead of disgrace you will rejoice in your inheritance . . . and everlasting joy will be yours" (Isaiah 61:7).

Shame needs to be uprooted and tossed away. True healing can exist only when shame is removed, all the way down to its roots.

The Nitty Gritty on Shame

It's important for you to recognize how shame operates in your life. Many noted psychologists have studied the affect of shame and have discovered numerous physical characteristics: blushing or flushing of the cheeks and neck, downward cast or darting eyes, rounded shoulders, slack posture, and a lowered head.

We know, however, that shame can also be sneaky. Shameful feelings can permeate our self-worth so profoundly that many survivors resort to deviant behaviors to try to cover up or overcompensate for wounded feelings.

But behind bad-girl or wild-child personas live hurting girls with shame-clad identities. Their behavior is a mirror of the way they feel about themselves and assume that others also see and feel about them.

As the psychologist Dr. Robert D. Stolorow puts it, "In some *accommodative patterns*, serving or performing becomes a way of substituting for a missing sense of inherent value and thereby maintaining a connection with a viewing other. *Defensive grandiosity and devaluation of, contempt for, rage at, or envy of a viewing other* can represent efforts to cover up or counteract unbearable shame."[11]

How Shame Operates

Shame wears many faces. Although you may not recognize some of the guises in which it manifests itself, it may be operating in a variety of ways in your life, some of which may include

- Self-loathing or self-chastisement—shame about your felt lack of value and worth.
- Fear of speaking or expressing opinions—shame about your perceived inadequacy.
- Discouragement—shame about a sense of failure or defeat.

- Timidity or shyness—shame in the presence of the unfamiliar.
- Self-awareness or self-consciousness—shame about perceived imperfect performance and ability; feeling overly conspicuous.
- Embarrassment—shame about the prospect of being seen or known by others.
- Depression—shame about being ashamed.
- Inferiority or inadequacy—general, all-encompassing shame.
- Contempt—shame for believing in hope.

How Shame Triggers

Shame is an ever-present reality, but there are times when the rush of shame sweeps over us more intensely. These moments can be triggered when

- Basic expectations or hopes are frustrated or crushed.
- Disappointments or perceived failures occur in important relationships.
- Relational bonds are perceived to be weakening.
- Perceived rejection or disapproval from needed others, such as a boss, spouse, or child, occurs.
- Needed others show disinterest.

Shame's Traveling Companions

Shame is the grandmother in the family of related emotions and consequences that include alienation, secrecy, loneliness, inferiority, and perfectionism. Shame is also at the root of many psychological disorders, such as depression, paranoia, addiction, and narcissistic conditions. Shame is further connected to eating and sexual disorders.

To Know and Be Known

"Search me, O God, and know my heart; test me and know my anxious thoughts. See . . . me" (Psalm 139:23–24, emphasis mine).

Have you longed for intimacy? Do you wonder what it must be like to be fully known by someone else who loves you?

One of the most beautiful of life's experiences is found in intimacy—"to know and to be known." Longing for that closeness isn't wrong; in fact, it's from God. Our Creator designed and wired us as human beings to enjoy transparency and closeness with each other—to be fully known without *feeling shame or judgment.* In fact, it is only within this intimate bond of acceptance (from God and others) that we can experience the true fullness of joy God desires for us.

However, sin made its debut in the world and messed up God's plan for intimacy. In the garden on that fateful day Satan crept in and beguiled humans (Genesis 3). Man and woman succumbed to his deception, and in one nibble of the forbidden fruit the guilty pair forfeited their purity and freedom. Shame, ever opportunistic, swooshed in to fill the void, and the humans ran for cover to conceal their true selves. They attempted to hide from the eyes of God, and from one another. Innocence was forever lost, and shame was born.

Still today shame cloaks our identity.

Our human desires didn't change—they were only tripped up by fear. We long for love as ardently as ever. We were created with a yearning to be known and accepted for who we truly are. Yet we deflect the very intimacy we crave. We run for cover, fearing, to our very core, the prospect of being exposed, while our faces flush with shame. Such is the fear of "in-to-me-see" (intimacy).

In Psalm 139 we are allowed to listen in on the intimate pleas of a terrified survivor. We hear David's heart cry, "See me! Know me!" The psalmist's raw soul longing burned like fire in his belly. He pleaded, "Lord, let your eyes search me, penetrating into the depths of my being. I need you to come close. I want no secrets from you, God. I long to have your undivided attention. I want to be known by You" (paraphrase mine).

Amazing!

How many of us are willing to invite a spiritual x-ray from an all-seeing God? David found the secret to ending shame in his life—friendship with God. When he met God, he encountered Love. And Grace, mercy, and acceptance.

David, known in perpetuity as a *man after God's own heart*, was also a man who had slept with another's wife, had a child with her, and dispatched the husband to certain death on the front lines of battle. Still, incredibly, he felt comfortable with God's all-knowing eyes searching his heart (check out Acts 13:22). And after God's search? David saw himself just as God saw him. Ponder again his own wondering words: "I praise you because I am fearfully and wonderfully made; your works are wonderful, I know that full well" (Psalm 139:14).

Shame cannot survive in the presence of God's love. For shame, at its root, is fear of exposure. And *perfect love casts out all fear.*

God is safe. He sees you and loves you, and He longs to eradicate the shame that is robbing you of the fullness of life He offers.

Listen to His words to His Old Testament servant Joshua: "Today I have rolled away the shame of your slavery in Egypt" (Joshua 5:9, NLT).

Roadside Check-up

In a quiet moment ask the Holy Spirit to guide you in this prayer: "Lord God, thank You for seeing me, knowing me, and finding me blameless. When You look at me, You see me through the lens of the sacrifice of Your own Son, Jesus Christ. Because of His blood shed for me, I stand before You whole, cleansed, beautiful, and pure. Today I see myself as You see me—cherished and accepted. I emerge from hiding and stand in Your glorious light. I shed my garments of shame and refuse to wear them any longer. Set me free from shame. In Jesus' name, Amen."

SILENCING THE TRASH TALK
Hushing Your Internal Critic

Sticks and stones may break my bones, but words will never leave me.
They will plague me for life, crush my spirit, and eventually destroy me.
—LOUISE

Many of us have heard the immortalized childhood cliché, popular through some point in the sixties when its falsity became evident, "Sticks and stone can break my bones, but words can never hurt me." In today's culture, for sure, this childhood ditty is accepted as patently untrue. Words not only *can and do* hurt and sting, but negative labels and criticism can destroy our self-esteem and decimate our confidence.

As a woman wounded by sexual abuse, you've probably been struck by negative words. Women in a sexual assault support group combined their experiences to share this list of terms that have haunted them:

ugly ◆ dirty ◆ slut ◆ stupid ◆ crazy ◆ whore ◆ ignorant ◆ clumsy ◆ fat ◆ smelly ◆ damaged goods ◆ head-case ◆ witch ◆ unwanted ◆ pest ◆ boring ◆ unattractive ◆ lazy ◆ seductive child ◆ liar ◆ conniving ◆ sex object ◆ good-for-nothing ◆ sad ◆ unforgiveable ◆ unloved ◆ mental ◆ gross ◆ defective ◆ hated by God ◆ useless

If you've been called any of those names or others like them, you know first-hand the damage they can do to your soul. If we internalize shaming words, we progress from hearing destructive words to believing we *are* those terms—that they somehow epitomize our essence. And once we believe wounding words—spoken by others or ourselves—those terms stalk us like a prison guard, intimidating us with what we perceive as a life sentence of defeat, worthlessness, and external control.

Sticks and stones may indeed break our bones, but words will do far worse: break our spirit.

Words

crush

our souls.

Words crushed Carol. She stared at the floor as she struggled to share her story: "As a child I had a toxic relationship with food. I found great comfort in eating. As a result, my weight put me in the 'above average' range on the scale, but I was far from obese.

"One day when I was about eight, I was singing and dancing and playing dress-up in the family room. My mother, a mean alcoholic recovering from a drunken binge, yelled for me to stop. Apparently, I was too happy.

"'But momma, I'm dancing for you,' I said.

"My mother shot back at me, 'Sit down and be quiet! Fat elephants don't dance!'"

Words

crush.

As noted psychologist Terry L. Ledford observes,

> Children are like sponges. If you place a sponge beside clear, pure water, it will soak that up. If you place it beside acid, it will soak that up as well. The sponge has no choice. It absorbs whatever it contacts. Children are no different. When they're exposed to encouragement and love, they absorb that. When they're exposed to criticism, neglect, or abuse, they absorb that as well. They have no choice.[12]

During my abusive childhood I soaked up many negative words and labels. Although my father didn't criticize me with name calling, he snapped at me and others sarcastically, jeered, and criticized. In his own words, this was "just his way." His speech was habitually drenched with satire and mockery. Although I laughed in apparent appreciation at his humor, I often felt afraid of him. If I didn't look or act appropriately, he ridiculed me and often publicly humiliated me for my alleged "stupidity."

I absorbed his dripping criticism like a sponge. Even when he wasn't speaking, his critical voice rang in my ears. I could see disapproval on his face and sense judgment in his mood. I developed a sixth sense and became adept at discerning the atmosphere he was setting in our home.

Is it safe today? Are my parents fighting? Has Dad been drinking?

I habitually assessed my surroundings. Most survivors of incest develop a sixth sense for gauging the emotional and physical safety of their environments in order to prepare for either fight or flight—or, in some cases, to freeze and please.

Eventually, I absorbed my father's attitudes of faultfinding and intolerance. His words came in my own mind to define me, and I was, to say the least, disenthralled with who I was.

I scolded myself before anyone else had a chance to put me down. I was quick to make self-effacing comments and to apologize for my actions and appearance. I found fault with everything I did and could think of little, if anything, positive to say about myself.

Birth of an Inner Critic

I developed the habit of self-criticism. When children are exposed to disparagement and faultfinding, ridicule and disapproval, they learn to initiate more of the same. The internal critic is born, and we enter into continuous negative dialogue with ourselves. You may be unaware of this incessant, ongoing self-talk, but it's there. Psychologists tell us that the average person experiences thousands of unconscious thoughts a day. For survivors, hundreds of critical, negative voices daily belittle us for our alleged flaws, failures, and frailties.

Here's how it works: as children, we're predisposed to believe we're inadequate. And indeed we are. We need others to teach, train, provide for, and "do for" us—without them we would be and remain helpless.

As a kid, I fell off my bike. I couldn't sharpen a pencil. I couldn't tie my shoe laces or work the toaster. I was inadequate. And normal. I wasn't supposed to know how to do those things when I was a young child.

As an adult I recognize that a lack of skill doesn't equate to incompetence, but as a child I hadn't developed that perspective. I didn't realize that skill comes with age, education, and experience. I feared that my inabilities constituted proof that I was somehow fundamentally defective.

The cycle of perfectionism began, and my inner critic was born. My self-criticism produced the very thing I dreaded—inadequacy. Because the less adequate I felt the more loudly my inner critic reminded me of my failings.

What about you? At what point does your inner critic show up? When you look in the mirror? When you try to master a new skill—or shudder at the very prospect of trying? When you blow up at your partner or yell at the kids? Maybe you've grown so accustomed to your inner critic that you don't even notice her—you've relegated her to the realm of some innocuous white noise in the background that nevertheless impinges on your consciousness and adversely affects your thought life. She's there, all right, demanding and demeaning as always—pushing you to do better and—a much more dicey proposition—to *be* better. Reprimanding you for being so lame. Because of abuse you've experienced rejection, abandonment, and fear, along with feelings of unworthiness and shame, of being unloved and unprotected. Your trauma negatively shaped your opinion of and beliefs about yourself, and those negative opinions and beliefs about who you are have generated feelings. Feelings produce choices, behavior, and words—in this case words that will crush your soul and break your spirit.

Psychologist Terry L. Ledford puts it this way: "If self-critical statements are a prominent part of your internal vocabulary, you need to understand that those statements are hurting your well-being. You can't have such thoughts without damaging your self-esteem and affecting your life choices. Self-critical thoughts often fuel depression and anxiety."[13]

If you engage in negative, critical, and toxic self-talk, your well-being is at stake. You'll remain stuck in the rut of shame and scorn. As your words shape your self-esteem, you'll have a difficult time trying to rise above a low opinion of yourself. Your healing will be waylaid, hijacked by damaging, self-defeating words.

Instead of postponing progress, why not silence the trash talk and hush your inner critic?

God wants to teach you a better vocabulary—words of blessing, promise, and hope.

Are you ready to learn a new way of talking to yourself?

Roadside Check-up

1. Listen to your self-talk. What is your internal critic saying to you?

2. Become aware of the things she says *to* you and *about* you. Are these words true? How do you know? Practice rephrasing those comments into a "redemptive voice."

3. Think about what kinds of things you're typically doing when your inner critic shows up. Perhaps this accusing voice fears your healing and recovery. Could this be an attack against you to keep you from freedom and hold you in defeat?

My life has been filled with terrible misfortunes, most of which have never happened. —MICHEL DE MONTAIGNE

◆   ◆   ◆

Reframing Your Mindset

It will be necessary for the recovering you to **learn concepts,** as well as **put them into practice by faith.** As you do, you'll begin to experience the transformation of your mind, thoughts, feelings, and behaviors. You'll develop a new mindset and replace negative narrative about yourself and about your past, present, and future life.

Brain science reveals that our centers of thought and memory often get "stuck" in the trauma we encounter. Even when we're exposed to positive experiences after a traumatic event, our brains often remain "trapped in the trauma," hurling us back in time to relive painful, negative, and destructive events. Trauma diminishes our brain's ability to overwrite the past with fresh data from the present. Our brain acts like a computer that doesn't possess the software to upload new information. Our mind holds on to the feelings, fears, and emotions of the past.[14] (We will explore this concept in detail in chapter 7.)

Not all is lost, however. Science also confirms for us what God's Word revealed thousands of years ago: our mind can be made new and change. Healing and transformation are possible. In the words of Paul's God-inspired invitation, "be transformed by the renewing of your mind" (Romans 12:2).

Reframing is a powerful transformative tool that helps us renew our minds. This process provides the software we need to reprogram them. But we must be willing to look at our stories—to recognize, sort through, engage, and evaluate our thought processes and memories—from a new angle. Taking ourselves out of the middle of our story, we can learn to place ourselves above it, in order to gain an objective, birds-eye view.

As Paul expressed in Ephesians 2:6, "God raised us up with Christ and seated us with him in the heavenly realms in Christ Jesus." In other words, through faith in Christ you have the advantage of being lifted above your circumstances. Former painful events have lost their power over you. Past trauma no longer defines you. From this divine vantage point you have the opportunity to reframe circumstances and situations in a manner that transcends, overrides, or overwrites your old story or interpretation. You can view hurtful experiences and upsetting interactions from a new angle and without interference from emotional obstacles. You can observe and respond instead of reacting as a victim.

Most survivors—myself included—would probably agree that this is true. Our abuse was horrific and degrading, and we've been doubly wounded in that we've developed self-critical inner dialogues that result in unrealistic expectations for and false judgments about ourselves since our abuse. Beyond the realities of the actual event(s), our thoughts and defeated inner dialogues have allowed the turbulent ripple effect of trauma to produce a victim mindset that has trickled (or freely flowed) into our adulthood.

It may come as a shock to learn that you have the power to stop this cycle!

The discipline of reframing involves identifying our unhelpful thoughts and replacing them with more positive or adaptive ones. This skill alone regularly helps me redirect the trajectory of my day—and eventually affects my larger life outlook. Instead of meditating on a negative thought sent to me as a text either from my own inner critic or from Satan's messenger, I deliberately capture and isolate the thought, reframe it to reflect God's truth, and then proclaim aloud what I alternately choose to believe and accept.

For example, when a critical thought comes to me—something like *You idiot. You just totally embarrassed yourself*—I recognize it as the voice of my inner critic and instantly reframe it: *That's not my thought and it isn't the truth. I have the mind of Christ. Today I was open and transparent for the glory of God.*

I experience many more positive, productive days than I once did. I'm able to work out the future I believe God has for me. Because good days lead to good months and good months to good years. Again in Paul's words, "We demolish arguments and every pretension that sets itself up against the knowledge of God, and we take captive every thought to make it obedient to Christ" (2 Corinthians 10:5).

Stinkin' Thinkin'

For us as abuse survivors, much of our inner dialogue is birthed from the cognitive distortions—thought contortions our mind persuades us to accept as true—we've formulated. When we tell ourselves falsities that sound rational and accurate, these lies and distortions reinforce our negative thinking and faulty belief systems. Our cognitive distortions perpetuate our feelings of worthlessness and keep us trapped and defeated. Since we know how to live as victims, we've successfully sabotaged our future and let ourselves "off the hook" when it comes to the prospect of dealing honestly with our past trauma and moving into wholeness.

Because a child is absolutely unprepared to process such a humiliating invasion as sexual abuse, our minds compensate with twisted logic and reasoning, forming distortions in our thinking processes.

Gloria's inner critic showed up daily. While driving to work each morning, she would frantically beat back a relentless pack of sneering voices.

"You're a failure at this job."

"No one at the office likes you."

"You never get any appreciation."

On and on the internal barrage continued, week after week. It was vicious. Debilitating. At night she lay awake thinking about how she might be able to better perform at work. Finally, Gloria collapsed under the exhaustion of a stress and anxiety disorder. She took a leave of absence but never returned to fulltime employment. As Gloria explained, "I couldn't silence the jeering of my inner critic, and I just got tired of the fight. It was easier to quit my job than to battle."

Cognitive distortions wreak havoc until the survivor identifies the thinking patterns and systematically eliminates them. With practice and intentionality, we can recognize and refute each of these distortions launched by a critical spirit. Reframing is an important step in ridding ourselves of crippling negative dialogues.

The most common distortions that originate from our inner critic are listed below. But remember, you can talk back, fight, and claim your true identity!

All-or-Nothing Reasoning

"People always interrupt me."

Abuse victims often develop black-or-white thinking patterns. They view circumstances and people as either good or bad, heroes or villains. They make few or no allowances for "both/and" scenarios, instead viewing life's circumstances as "either/or." They frequently use words like "always" or "never."

However, you can learn to reframe by replacing such sweeping generalities with modifying words or phrases like "sometimes, or "now and again." You can also benefit from thinking of counter-examples. Example: "While it's true that I'm sometimes interrupted, it's also true that many people listen to me intently and appreciate my point of view."

Over-Generalization
"Since I failed at this, I'll fail at everything."

Over-generalizing happens when we take an isolated event and make an all-encompassing assumption based on it, applying the generality to every subsequent event, person, or situation. We can learn to reframe when we remind ourselves that the next comparable situation may end in a totally different way. Example: "I didn't do well at it this time. But this is an isolated event. Next time I try something it will be a brand new experience."

Predicting a Negative Future
"I knew something terrible was going to happen! It always does."

Otherwise known as catastrophizing, this distorted paradigm habitually predicts a cataclysmic, impending disaster. Your mind magnifies and exaggerates every encounter. "Blow-ups" and emotionally dramatic episodes frequently occur, followed by incessant "If only . . . [things could be different]" modes of wistful and wishful thinking.

Continually bracing for a crisis foments within us incredible stress, anxiety, and health hazards.

Reframe your thoughts by reminding yourself that you cannot predict the future and that good, happy things are just as likely to happen as bad or sad events. Example: "I don't know what tomorrow may bring, but I know that with God I can handle whatever comes my way. Anyway, chances are it will be great!"

Filtering: Discounting the Positive
"Anyone can do what I do. I'm nothing special."

Filtering is a pattern of thinking that magnifies negative details while ignoring the positive. This technique deflects positive attention, minimizing your perceived value and discounting your accomplishments. This cognitive distortion decreases your confidence and massively decimates your self-esteem.

Reframe by accepting compliments and receiving reward, recognition, and self-gratification. Example: "I possess special skills in this area and am thankful that I enjoy doing this well. God has blessed me with wonderful talents."

Personalization

"If I hadn't been born, the cook would not have burned the meal."

When you believe that everything others do or say is in reaction to yourself, chances are you're struggling with a distortion called personalization. While it's good to take responsibility for *your* actions, if you believe that you're the cause for other people's hurt and pain, joy and success, you're assuming responsibility—and power—that just aren't yours. Reframe by reminding yourself that you aren't the cause of external events. Example: "Hey, remember: it isn't all about me. Things happen in this world, and I'm not responsible for them. The cook burned the dinner because the oven was too hot [or she forgot to set the timer or became distracted by loud voices outside, or whatever]."

Rejection

"I wasn't invited. I'm totally worthless. No one ever likes me."

The distortion here is that rejection—either real or perceived—always equates in your mind to your being worthless and inadequate. While rejection (or assumed rejection) can be painful, your perception is subjective. Who gets to decide what counts as rejection? By reframing, you may find that a missed opportunity was really a set-up for a greater one. And even actual rejection doesn't have to have a negative outcome. Example: "I'm not going to take rejection personally because I did my very best, and it's better to try than to do nothing at all. Plus, I believe that God has something even better in store for me. This missed opportunity will ultimately turn out for my good."

"Should" Thinking

"I should exercise and eat better. I'm so lazy."

Do you follow a rulebook full of ironclad directives concerning how you and other people ought to behave? If you become angry and irritable when people don't act as you think they should, or if you feel guilty and depressed because of your own behavior, you're probably dealing with "should" thinking. If you're regularly applying the words *should, must,* and *ought* to yourself and others, be warned that the emotional result of this distortion will be inappropriate anger and misplaced guilt.

Guilt-inducing manipulation and control through the application of "should" thinking can be reframed. Replace the *should have, ought to,* and *must do* with a mental review of potential positives for alternative behaviors. Example: "I usually enjoy how I feel after a good workout. I'd like to try to do it more often."

Cognitive distortions may present themselves in any combination of one or all of these categories, perhaps in conjunction with a few I haven't mentioned. The important fact is that, with effort, you can learn to recognize and change your stinkin' thinkin' and begin to eradicate it. Healing and freedom will flow as you renew your mind.

As you begin to tear down old belief systems, feelings, and thoughts and submit them to the light of God's Word, you're on your way to a new beginning.

◆　◆　◆

Roadside Check-up

Maintain a "Thought Journal." When your inner critic feeds you negative and critical thoughts, jot them down. This interrupts your destructive thoughts, allows you to objectively explore their validity (*Is this true? Why or why not?*), and invites you to reframe and answer back in a positive, truthful manner.

— *Part 2* —

DEMYSTIFYING THE PROBLEMS

Examining the Difficult Aftermath of Your Trauma

— 6 —

COPING WITH WOUNDS AND WEAPONS

Connecting Your Problems to the Trauma

God whispers to us in our pleasures . . . but shouts in our pains.
—C. S. LEWIS

I love the popular movie *Bruce Almighty*. In one comical scene the main character, Bruce, reaches his wits' end as mounting personal problems reach a boiling point and erupt.

Imagine with me a dreary night. Rain splashes in torrents over a blurry car windshield. Bruce, running from his pain, recklessly accelerates down a dark, slick road. As he drives, Bruce shoots up an S.O.S. to heaven—one feeble, last-resort plea for rescue. He pleads with God: "I need a sign. . . . Just give me a sign, God! Pleeease, God, I need help."

As he fervently prays, he passes one sign after another.

Big signs.

Bigger signs.

Billboards.

But ironically, Bruce continues to *plead for a sign*. Finally, a utility truck overflowing with highway safety signs pulls in front of him. The irony is beyond obvious. Everything for which Bruce asks God is smack dab in front of him. Still, Bruce doesn't recognize the signs.

We're a lot like Bruce.

We can't see the signs.

Or we won't

see the signs all around us

because we just aren't looking.

Danger Signs

Danger signs can be found everywhere in life, but we typically choose to ignore them—even when our wounded souls lie, inert, beneath the rubble of abuse.

We minimize our pain and turn to familiar coping skills.

"I'm okay," we gamely insist. "The pain isn't all that bad."

We declare that we've "forgiven" and are "fine" and that the negative effects of our abuse have magically slipped "into the past."

We pretend we haven't been affected by sexual abuse because the thought makes us feel safe—anything to deceive ourselves into thinking we can control our lives and not be hurt again. We tell ourselves, "That happened years ago. By now I must be over it."

But that doesn't work either. Eventually our denial shatters because we've ignored the signs that have been there all along:

Wounds.

Hurts.

Addictions.

Dependencies.

Anger.

Ailments.

When will we open our eyes and see that we're *not* all right?

The signs are right in front of us if we'll just look.

DANGER
Your current problems may be directly related to your abusive past.

If you've experienced sexual trauma and have never dealt with it, chances are you're struggling in some area of your life. During the process of healing you will make connections between ongoing struggles and past sexual abuse.

Maybe you don't want to acknowledge your current hang-ups and hurts, but they're probably glaringly obvious to others. You're afraid of the pain. I get it. I wish I could tell you that pain weren't a part of healing, but it is. Healing pain, however, won't devour you. It isn't your enemy. Emotional discomfort is a wake-up call alerting you to brokenness in your life. Without pain, most of us ignore, postpone, procrastinate, and put off altogether the pursuit of healing.

You see, unprocessed sexual trauma will cling to you like a frightened infant grips its mother. If you're going to walk in healing and freedom, you need to relinquish your ineffective coping skills and let go of your defensive armor.

In chapter 3 I asked you to take a "Fearless Moral Inventory." The purpose of the inventory was to help you recognize your trauma aftermath and how it operates in your life. In this chapter we will review the ground we've already covered, discover and abandon faulty coping skills and defense mechanisms, and respond to pain with healthy skills.

◆　◆　◆

Coping with Wounds

A litany of injuries stems from childhood sexual abuse. The catalogue of pain symptoms is common to many types of early childhood trauma, but unique problems exist for the little girl who has suffered sexual trauma and abuse. Her wounds go very deep.

First, let's be clear on what we mean by the term "sexual abuse."

The Reality of Abuse

Many people mistakenly believe that sexual abuse, including childhood sexual abuse, is limited to intercourse or penetration. But many forms exist, and no matter which kind you've experienced the exploitation has inflicted pain and injury on your psyche.

The three basic categories of abuse include touching, non-touching, and exploitation.

Touching includes
- Fondling.
- Forcing a child to touch an adult's sexual organs.
- Inappropriate touching, pinching, or tickling.
- Forcing another to kiss or to French kiss.
- Forcing another to perform oral or anal sex.
- Using fingers or objects to penetrate a child's vagina or anus.
- Rape.

Non-touching includes
- Voyeurism—watching a child undress or take a bath.
- Exposure—showing a child an adult's sexual organs.
- Masturbating in front of a child.
- Forcing a child to watch pornography.
- Sexual intercourse in front of a child.

Exploitation includes
- Taking pictures of a naked child.
- Using a child for pornography.
- Forcing a child into prostitution.

Regardless of what form it may take, sexual abuse is a horrific invasion. The child's will is overthrown, her voice silenced, and her body ravaged. Yet many people falsely believe that the "degree" of abuse determines the severity of its impact on the survivor.

"It is often assumed that touching and fondling of the breasts and genital area is less traumatic than vaginal or rectal penetration or oral sex. Not only is this assumption untrue, but other forms of non-touching sexual abuse can be equally devastating from the child's point of view."[15]

Sexual abuse, in any degree, wounds its victims. It involves power, control, and manipulation and is, therefore, not a crime of lust or passion but a violent crime of aggression and domination that injures.

If you've experienced *any* form of sexual molestation, then you've experienced physical, mental, and psychological molestation. During your violation your mind underwent a terrible and frightening experience—an isolating experience.

No one was there to talk you through the experience.

No on was present to comfort you.

No one was with you to care for your injuries.

You felt totally alone.

Perhaps you even felt as though God had turned His back on you.

◆   ◆   ◆

Sexual abuse changed you.

Not just emotionally and psychologically, but biologically as well. Your brain chemistry shifted as you experienced trauma. (We'll discuss this further in the next chapter.)

Survivors deal with a maelstrom of consequences and injuries, many of which don't show up until a woman reaches middle age. If you identify with any of the following symptoms, you may want to consider how they could be linked to your sexual abuse trauma:

- Shame and guilt
- Feelings of worthlessness and damaged self-esteem
- Fear, anxiety, and panic attacks
- Sleep disturbances
- Eating disorders
- Flashbacks and impaired memory
- Fear of trust and intimacy
- Depression and suicidal thoughts
- Mood disorders
- Personality disorders
- Addictions and compulsions
- Promiscuity and sexual dysfunction
- Self-destructiveness
- Codependence
- Unexplained pain and/or chronic pain

+ Migraines
+ Stomach ailments and ulcers
+ Gastrointestinal issues

We don't always make the connection between our symptoms and our traumatic past. But long after we've suppressed our memories, denied any further negative impact, or claimed our magical recovery, sexual abuse complicates and riddles our lives with its long-term effects.

In her book *Hope, Healing, and Help for Survivors of Sexual Abuse* Sue Cameron points out that

> Survivors may fail to link the negative symptoms they experience in their daily lives with the fact that they were sexually abused. But making the connection is a critical step in healing. Sexual abuse injures us in many ways—emotionally, mentally, relationally, and sometimes physically. We don't always comprehend the long-term influences or the exact ways we are affected by past trauma, but the Lord does.[16]

When you make the connection between your past and your current ailments and other difficulties, you receive a beautiful gift: hope. You don't have to be sick for the rest of your life. You don't have to live stuck, depressed, and withdrawn. Healing is possible for you.

But this revelation requires action. What will you do with the discoveries you make?

Roadside Check-up

1. As you prayerfully consider items on the List of Injuries, consider which symptoms you identify with. Write them down if you find it helpful.

2. In what ways do you feel these symptoms may be connected to your sexual abuse trauma?

3. Ask the Lord to reveal which of your feelings, beliefs, or fears may be associated with your symptoms. For example, you may declare that you've forgiven and that your ordeal is over, but whenever you see a little girl walking hand-in-hand with her grandfather you experience a panic attack.

4. Pray: "Dear Lord Jesus, show me the areas in which I'm still broken. Expose the hidden secrets of pain that keep me afflicted with symptoms and sickness, and deliver me from the grip of trauma so I can find healing. In Jesus' name, Amen."

◆   ◆   ◆

Mad Skills and Defense Strategies

Elizabeth's exuberant, melodious voice emanated joy and giggles to those around her. As we chopped veggies at my kitchen sink, we were soon both bent over holding our stomachs, laughing in hysterics. Elizabeth was always the comedian.

Always.

But when the laughter stopped, Liz faced a reality she didn't want to confront.

"If I ever stop laughing I'll die in anguish," she told me as she turned toward my kitchen window. "The past is over. But I can't face it, and I won't ever speak of it again."

The heinous details of Elizabeth's abuse were so far beyond her comprehension that she had resorted to a coping skill—humor—to help her to function day-to-day and to suppress her pain.

When a woman has been abused and her senses overloaded, anxiety overwhelms her, and the pain becomes too intense to handle. Chemicals change in the brain, causing her to feel off balance and out of control. According to Sydney Youngerman-Cole and Katy E. Magee, "Many mental health problems begin when physical stress or emotional stress triggers chemical changes in your brain."[17]

In an attempt to survive, maintain control, and handle anxiety and stress, women either consciously or subconsciously create coping skills and defense mechanisms. These may work while the abuse is ongoing or immediately afterward. At the time they make sense and may even save your life. But using these coping skills, defense mechanisms, masks, and shields as a way to live a protected life long after the abuse is over is unhealthy and dangerous. These patterns of behavior are a substitute for true healing and recovery and are tragically less than what God has planned for you.

Coping Skills or Copping Out?

Coping refers to expending intentional, conscious effort to manage, master, or minimize internal stress, pain, or conflict. *Coping skills* deploy intentional effort to neutralize stress. In the above illustration Elizabeth refined and adapted the coping skill of humor as a mechanism for subduing her internal turmoil.

Coping strategies are not inherently negative. They may help us overcome difficult circumstances and assist us in our quest for a return to health and wellness. But other coping strategies can be destructive. While they may offer a temporary solution to stress, they offer no permanent healing from emotional injury. Resorting to bad or ineffective coping skills can keep women stuck in their woundedness and stalled in terms of their potential for personal, emotional, spiritual, and relational growth.

Effective coping skills that promote health and healing include

1. Physical activity
2. Good nutrition
3. Reading and learning
4. Spiritual life in God
5. Meditation and deep breathing exercises
6. Laughter
7. Prayer
8. Time for yourself
9. Rest and relaxation

10. Friendships
11. Hobbies and recreation

Destructive coping skills that serve only to mask pain include

+ Drugs
+ Alcohol
+ Stimulants
+ Binge eating
+ Ignoring problems / avoidance
+ Sedation
+ Excessive working
+ Excessive sleep
+ Holding on to hurts and storing up offenses
+ Denial
+ Self-mutilation

If you recognize any of these negative coping skills at work in your life, I encourage you to find a counselor and work through these issues together. It's possible that you're using one or more of these strategies to stomp down your past pain to keep it out of your conscious mind. Make a promise to yourself that you'll explore a healthier way to face life. Be willing to separate from false security and reach for true freedom.

Defense Mechanisms and Escaping Reality

Have you ever been driving along when you slipped into a pervasive daydream? The next thing you knew you'd missed your exit and perhaps even driven far past your intended destination.

I hope this happens to people other than just me!

We sigh and think, *Wow, I must've been on auto-pilot.* Without conscious awareness on our part we've slipped out of our present reality and "gone away" to a more comfortable place somewhere in our mind.

Defense mechanisms are thought to be the mind's *largely unconscious auto-pilot tactics.* Our minds initially developed this strategy to distance and safeguard us from feelings, thoughts, activities, or memories that were at the time beyond our coping ability. Such defense mechanisms are activated when we come under extreme stress and anxiety. Defense mechanisms, as survival instruments, are gifts from God for our protection.

For example: Your spouse comes home from work and tells you that he wants to be intimate, but you struggle with the whole sex thing. Your mind unconsciously dismisses his request in order to avoid the dreaded and feared interlude. That defense mechanism is *forgetting.*

Another example can be seen in Bonita's story. The sexual abuse committed against her was frequent and pervasive. At six years old she regularly hid under her makeshift bed—made of two file cabinets, a sheet of plywood and a mattress—to avoid being raped. But night after night she was dragged out from underneath the "bed" and forced to perform sexual acts on her uncle. One night little Bonita made a discovery: "I pretended I was a mermaid who could dive off the side of the bed and float in the ocean. By immersing myself in the waters of imagination, I realized I could mentally escape my sexual torture. I endured every episode of hellish molestation the same way."

Eventually Bonita's *escape from reality* turned into a defense mechanism known as *splitting,* or *dissociation*—deliberate mental disconnection from the present time, place, and reality in order to allow a false self to take over. Still today, whenever the adult Bonita faces uncomfortable situations she dissociates from reality and emotionally escapes to a safer place. (More on dissociation follows in the next chapter.)

Some defense methods do indeed serve a vital and Rnecessary purpose during abuse, but dangers arise when we rely on defense mechanisms as a replacement for our healing, growth, and development following the trauma. Dysfunctional defense systems wreak havoc in terms of our emotional and psychological wellness. At first defense techniques help us avoid intrusive emotions for which we lack the emotional reserves to deal. But eventually the defense tactic takes over, suppressing all of our emotions and feelings. Suppressed emotions lead to psychological and physical problems. Troubling symptoms damage our core self and increase our dependency on habits, addictions, mood-altering drugs, and fantasies, impairing our ability to function. This loss of functionality leads to broken relationships, loss of intimacy, and lack of trust. In the end we become prisoner to our own contrived methods of escape.

Some of the most common defense mechanisms used by sexual abuse survivors include

+ **Forgetting.** Releasing important information from our minds as a way of avoidance. "If I can't remember, I won't have to do it."
+ **Denial,** a refusal to admit or recognize reality. Even in the face of incontrovertible facts and evidence, people in denial are unable or unwilling to accept truth. When facts cannot be avoided, denial minimizes the importance of an issue.
+ **Repression.** This unconscious tactic acts to keep information out of the conscious mind. Because memories don't truly disappear they continue to influence our behavior; therefore, a survivor feels disconnected from her behavior and her understanding of why she feels and acts in the way she does.
+ **Suppression.** Like the above examples, we unconsciously force unwanted information away from our awareness and push it underground.
+ **Rationalization,** explaining an unacceptable behavior or feeling in a logical manner, avoiding the true reasons for the behavior; false reasoning.
+ **Passive-aggression,** indirectly expressing and directing anger, all the while insisting that we're "fine."
+ **Dissociation.** When trauma overwhelms the personality and one's ability to process, the core person splits off from herself, sending a representation of the self—a substitute—to be present during the stressful situation. People who use dissociation often have a disconnected view of life and feel as though they're floating above the situation, looking down and watching instead of being actively present.
+ **Compartmentalization,** a lesser form of dissociation, wherein part of one's self operates under a separate set of values. The individual

resorting to this technique keeps the parallel value systems distinct and nonintegrated, while remaining unconscious of the cognitive dissonance.

+ **Projection**, attributing our own undesired or unacceptable thoughts, feelings, or impulses to another person. Projection is often responsible for our lack of acknowledgment of or insight into our own motivations and feelings. If you're angry with someone, for example, you might instead believe that he or she is angry with you. Projection works by allowing you to express the feeling or impulse while pinning it on another.

+ **Reaction Formation**, converting unwanted or dangerous thoughts, feelings, or impulses into the opposite thought or feeling. When you are incapable of expressing the negative emotions of anger and unhappiness, for example, you may instead become gracious and kind to demonstrate your lack of anger and unhappiness.

+ **Displacement**, taking out our frustrations, feelings, and impulses on people or objects that are less threatening. Displaced aggression is most common. Instead of expressing anger in ways that could lead to negative consequences, we direct our anger toward someone or something that poses no threat. Example: I'm angry with my boss, so I kick the cat.

+ **Acting Out**. Here we cope with stress and anxiety by participating in actions—either constructive or destructive—rather than reflecting on internal feelings.

+ **Affiliation**. We garner support and turn to others to meet our needs.

+ **Aim Inhibition**, accepting a modified and lesser form of our original goal. Example: I wanted to be a professional singer, but instead I give voice lessons.

+ **Altruism**, fulfilling our own needs by taking care of others. Manifestations may include obsessive caretaking or serving or martyrdom.

+ **Compensation**, overachieving in one area to compensate for perceived failures in another.

+ **Humor**, using jokes, laughter, and humor to avoid the painful aspects of a situation or memory. This approach may include satire and self-abasement.

Overuse of defense mechanisms will impede your healing and recovery. By deadening your awareness to your true, root issues, your defense tactics interfere with your healthy, normal, and functional living and stall the mature development of your personality, which God created to be fully alive and free. Isn't it time to uncover these unconscious, destructive mechanisms so that you can choose better, healthier ways of living?

The true *you* wants to emerge.

So lay down your weapons.

God's got you.

Roadside Check-up

1. Prayerfully consider the above list. Many of these defense mechanisms are expressed subconsciously. Ask the Holy Spirit to reveal those that may be functioning in you.

2. Write down what you have discovered. In what ways do you see yourself employing defense mechanisms? As you consider your list, do you see a recurring theme, such as fear, avoidance, or control?

3. What do you think would change in your life if you were to release those defensive weapons?

DISCOVERING THAT IT ISN'T OVER WHEN IT'S OVER
Understanding Post-Traumatic Stress Syndrome

Trauma is personal. It does not disappear if it is not validated. When it is ignored or invalidated the silent screams continue internally heard only by the one held captive. When someone enters the pain and hears the screams healing can begin. —DANIELLE BERNOCK, *Emerging with Wings*

Most survivors of sexual violence experience anxiety, depression, stress, and fear because those responses are normal. But these feelings and symptoms can become intense and persistent, to the point of interrupting day-to-day life. When they manifest themselves through more than occasional episodes, the condition is known as post-traumatic stress disorder (PTSD).

PTSD Is Not Just about Veterans

Most people associate PTSD with soldiers returning from war who often come home *different*. Our veterans have often witnessed inexpressible horror, bloodshed, and desolation. They leave the war behind, but the war does not leave them. This is because many of them struggle with a condition called Post-Traumatic Stress Disorder (PTSD), an anxiety disorder that occurs when a traumatic event overwhelms the brain's ability to cope. This description applies to survivors of any type of trauma, including the following:

natural disasters	technological disasters
pre-birth child loss	adoption
abandonment	domestic violence
sexual abuse	physical abuse
emotional abuse	job-related trauma (e.g., law enforcement, first responders, etc.)

People with PTSD experience intense feelings of stress, fear, anxiety, and nervousness. They feel as though they are constantly in danger, making it difficult for them to function in everyday life.

PTSD Realities

According to the National Center for PTSD:

+ Trauma is common in women.
+ Five out of ten women will experience a traumatic event in their lifetime.
+ One out of three women will experience sexual assault in their lifetime.
+ Women are also more likely to be neglected or abused in childhood, to experience domestic violence, or to have a loved one suddenly die.
+ Women tend to experience different traumas from men but report the same symptoms of PTSD, though some symptoms are more common among women.
+ In instances of sexual assault, women's reactions are similar to those of male combat veterans.
+ Women are more than twice as likely to develop PTSD than men. This is due, in part, to the fact that sexual assault more than any other event is likely to cause PTSD.
+ Women appear to be more likely to blame themselves for trauma experiences than are men.[18]

Though survivors react differently, all exhibit three main symptoms of PTSD:

+ **Re-experiencing:** feeling as though you are reliving the event through flashbacks, dreams, or intrusive thoughts.
+ **Avoidance:** either intentionally or subconsciously changing your behavior to avoid scenarios associated with the event or losing interest in activities you used to enjoy.

+ **Hyper-arousal:** feeling "on edge" all of the time, having difficulty sleeping, being easily startled, or being prone to sudden outbursts.[19]

Why Trauma Is So Traumatic

Many abused children cling to the hope that growing up will bring them escape and freedom. But the personality formed in an environment of coercive control doesn't adapt well to adult life. The survivor enters adulthood with fundamental problems in the areas of trust, autonomy, and initiative and with altered thinking patterns. She approaches the tasks of early adulthood—establishing independence and intimacy—burdened by major impairments in issues involving self-care, cognition, memory, identity, and the capacity to form stable relationships. She is still a prisoner of her childhood; attempting to create a new life, she reencounters the trauma."[20]

No Room under the Rug

Sweeping your pain under the rug doesn't work.

Telling yourself to "just get over it" doesn't help.

Exerting your will to be better doesn't make you whole.

If these techniques worked, you'd be free by now—unless you derive satisfaction or comfort from being in a perpetual state of "victimhood." If that's true for you—as it was for me (something I recognized in hindsight)—it's additional evidence that you haven't fully recovered.

Ignoring your suffering won't make it disappear.

But what if I told you that your life could be more than mere existence—that you could live free of a victim mindset and the resulting consequences because you no longer believed the lie that *you are permanently "damaged-goods"*?

It's true.

This better life includes valuing yourself and believing—without associated guilt—that what happened to you was significant and deserves attention. You are worthy of the time and investment of healing. You aren't overstating the impact of your sexual abuse when you pause to confront your trauma head-on.

People often make thoughtless comments, such as "Things happen. Just deal with it." Or "I've had junk happen to me as a kid, too, and you don't see me falling apart." These remarks and others like them send a message inferring that it's a waste of time to revisit the past, but nothing could be further from the truth.

Ignore the ignorance and pursue your wholeness.

Effects of Sexual Abuse

Sexual abuse traumatizes survivors in different ways. As you read through the following examples, evaluate the degree to which each may be true of you.

Emotional Effects

Perhaps your mother spoke to you in a harsh tone and called you degrading names during your childhood abuse. For you as an adult, when someone's tone begins to escalate, you associate the present with your past abuse.

Physical Effects

If, when you were young, your perpetrator violated your face in some way during your abuse, you may be fearful of medical procedures during which your face may be covered or restrained.

Mental Effects

If you were made to feel unworthy or ugly or were threatened, tortured, or in other ways mentally or emotionally abused, you may return to those memories and survival behaviors when you believe that others are trying to control you or that your safety is at risk.

Biological Effect

When a terrifying event such as sexual abuse happens to someone, the stress can be so overwhelming that it overrides the person's ability to cope or process the trauma. One side of the brain freezes, so the trauma becomes "trapped" and can't be given an ending and filed in proper sequence. The biological chemistry of the trauma causes the event to be processed only partially—by only half of the brain.

Catatonic Immobility
At times the brain responds to extreme trauma by shutting down to external stimuli and internal commands, producing catatonic immobility.

What about Memories?

Not everyone can remember their abuse. The actual experience of sexual abuse is so horrifying, so stressful and overwhelming, that it's common for children to push the encounter into the deep recesses of their soul, not to be consciously recalled for years. They survive by disconnecting and blocking out any awareness of the abuse in order to function and maintain a façade of normalcy.

Blocking memories can temporarily protect children emotionally, psychologically, relationally, and in many other ways. But while blocking memories may provide protection for a time, repressed memories frequently return—often five, ten, or even dozens of years later. Frequently, once a person is out of danger and feels assured of their safety—either consciously or unconsciously—forgotten past memories intrude into the present. And when those memories come, they demand attention.

But the question remains: "If memories are buried, why not leave them buried?" The answer is simple: buried memories hold power.

They have the potential to generate damaging symptoms like anxiety, low self-esteem, depression, chronic pain, relational dysfunction, substance abuse, self-mutilation, and suicidal ideation. Sometimes survivors mistakenly believe that the symptoms themselves are the source of the problem. But symptoms simply point to their source: unresolved sexual trauma. Unless the memory is confronted, a woman may continue to act out, unaware of the cause of her depression or anxiety.

One woman I met, Catherine, cried in anguish as she shared. Cat, as she liked to be called, was plagued by memories that would pop into her mind, seemingly unprompted and without warning. She was afraid to close her eyes, even to fall asleep at night. Her confusion was revealed by her questions. Listen to our back-and-forth dialogue:

"Why now? After all these years, why do I have to face my past now?"

"Why *not* now? When did you plan to deal with your abuse?"

"Why, never, of course. At least that's what my counselor told me."

I wondered where she'd received such poor advice. Cat went on to tell me the story: "When I was in my twenties, I went to see a counselor. I was experiencing depression, anxiety, and fear. I thought it might be due to my past sexual abuse. But when my therapist asked me what happened, I said I didn't remember most of it."

That's when the counselor told Cat that God had given her a great gift: amnesia. "Keep the memories buried and go on." And for the next thirty years that's exactly what she did.

Now, at the age of fifty-two, her suppressed and forbidden memories were trying to break through to her conscious mind.

A memory may resurface in many ways. In his book *When a Man You Love Was Abused*, Cecil Murphey talks about several different types of memories that can occur:

1. *Visual Memories.* Images can be clear or vague and blurry, but distinct enough to cause the woman to remember and sometimes relive the abuse as though it were happening all over again.
2. *Auditory Memories.* A memory can be triggered by sounds: music, heavy breathing, whistling, footsteps, a door opening, or other noises associated with the event(s).
3. *Sensory Memories.* Memories can be triggered by certain smells, like toothpaste, alcohol, colognes, or body odor. A woman may freak out when she smells the brand of men's cologne her perpetrator wore.
4. *Body Memories.* Just as an athlete's muscles "remember" because of repetition and training, our bodies retain memories due to reoccurring and repetitive sensations. In the same way that other memories resurface, repressed body memories can occur spontaneously. Some survivors experience pain or sensations flowing over their genitals at

unexplained, seemingly random times. If you experience phantom pains in your breasts or genitals, know that you aren't crazy. Your body is re-experiencing trauma, even though you may have no cognitive memory of it.

5. *Emotional Memories.* It's possible for survivors to experience emotions (like feeling sad for no apparent reason) and react to triggers (perhaps newscasts or other stimuli) without understanding that these responses are connected to the sexual trauma of their past. Feeling powerless for whatever reason can trigger memories. When an event calls up the feeling of being out of control, the survivor can have memories or experience flashbacks that force them to relive their trauma.[21]

Triggers

A trigger occurs when an outward stimulus or catalyst causes an emotional or physical reaction. When a survivor is triggered, she often feels disoriented and can have trouble distinguishing the present from the past. Triggers can cause anxiety, startle responses, fear, and other symptoms.

As one survivor put it, "When I'm triggered, I'm instantly catapulted into the past. I emotionally crash to the ground, and there's no mat."

A trigger can be anything—a certain smell, a touch, a sound—and survivors can't know in advance when they'll come. A woman can be triggered by the smell of alcohol because her abuser was drunk when he attacked her. The nice old man who greets at the church on Sunday mornings smells like Old Spice. She reacts in an instant because Grandpa, who molested her, wore Old Spice. Another woman bristles when her hairdresser touches her hair. A female relative caressed her hair before she fondled her.

Some women are triggered by certain words. Being told to "relax" triggers me. My abuser used that expression. When I hear it I involuntarily stiffen up, a far cry from relaxing. Another common verbal trigger for female survivors is the phrase "I love you." Abusers are notorious for using this one. The abuse survivor may have a hard time hearing her husband declare "I love you" and a harder time understanding what he means when he says it.

It's important for us as survivors to understand our triggers. Without that knowledge we're apt to think, "I don't like my hairdresser; she gives me the creeps." Instead of recognizing our sensitivity we change hairdressers, churches, and partners. In an effort to stifle the pain, survivors run from triggers, when, instead, we need to look inside for healing.

A goal of therapy is to diffuse the intensity and power of triggers. One way we do that is by working with the counselor to identify specific triggers. It's unwise (and in many cases nearly impossible) to avoid them altogether; exposing ourselves to them little by little allows us to learn and practice new responses.

If you're a friend or spouse who's reading this book, be aware that your loved one may need your assurance as she goes through this process.

- Help her develop positive self-talk that says, *I'm okay. I can handle it today. I'm not a helpless child but a healthy adult.*
- You can also support her by helping her evaluate her experience. You might ask such questions as "What was the trigger? What were you feeling? What can you do for yourself this time that you couldn't do before?"
- Questions like these can be effective in helping her safely ride the wave of emotion and fear and can diffuse the magnitude of the trigger the next time.

The intimate sexual experience is a virtual landmine for triggers. If you're her sexual partner, take the time to investigate the sexual triggers in her life. Many couples are caught off guard when their evening of candles and romance turn into a chaotic, dark, and stormy night. Until you find and dismantle her triggers, your intimate life together may remain unaccountably tempestuous.

Flashbacks

Flashbacks are sudden memories that intrude into our present, often precipitated by a trigger. Flashbacks can consist of blurry and fuzzy images or be clear, dramatic, and precise pictures. These abrupt flashes of recollection transport survivors back to the past, forcing them to relive or re-experience their trauma.

Although flashbacks are disruptive and alarming, we shouldn't fear them. Flashbacks can be a positive sign that we're moving toward healing. Our psyche is telling us, "I'm ready to recall and process the past." Rather than hastily dismissing scenes from the past, survivors are wise to "flow" with the memory and allow the flashback to sweep, unimpeded, over them. Once we understand that we're having flashbacks of our past, their fearful power may diminish.

My flashbacks, never clear, were often sensory memories. I couldn't see real images, but I felt the associated emotions and sensations. The flash could come in an instant and last for only a few seconds, but when it passed I was left feeling weak and nauseous and was drenched with perspiration. At first I wasn't sure what was happening, and I described the feeling as a *déjà vu* experience, something that felt vaguely familiar. I now understand that this was a memory trying to push its way to the surface.

One woman in the recovery process reported that she kept having flashes of what she thought was a blanket coming down on top of her, covering her face and smothering her. As the flashbacks continued, they increased in length and clarity until she had a clear picture. The blanket was the flannel shirt of the man who had molested her. He had lain on her and forced himself into her face.

"I couldn't breathe," she told me. "I tried to move, but every time I did he pushed himself deeper into me." The flashback was painful, and the full memory was even more horrible. But once she processed the memory the flashback stopped, and she began to heal.

The following tips for managing flashbacks are suggested by Peter Walker:

+ Tell yourself, "This is a flashback." Flashbacks take us into a part of ourselves that feels helpless and hopeless. Remind yourself that past memories can't hurt you now.
+ Reassure yourself that though you feel afraid you aren't in danger.

+ Acknowledge your right to set healthy boundaries. You will no longer let anyone mistreat you. You will leave dangerous situations and report abuse and unfair treatment.

+ Reassure your Inner Child. Tell her that you love her unconditionally and that she can come to you when she feels afraid.

+ Address fatalistic thinking. You *can* change your painful past. The flashback will pass. You haven't been abandoned.

+ Remind yourself that you're an adult with friends, resources, and skills that you didn't have as a child to protect you.

+ Ground yourself to ease back into your body. Fear draws us into dissociation, anger, irrational worry, and numbing out. Breathe deeply, asking each of your muscle groups to relax, find a safe place to unwind and self-soothe, wrap up in a blanket, take a nap, or stroke your pet.

+ Resist your Inner Critic's voice insisting that the situation needs to be drastic and catastrophic. Squelch such thoughts and end the cycle of exaggerating danger and making situations appear catastrophic. Refuse to shame, blame, or hate yourself.

+ Say NO to self-criticism.

+ Replace negative thinking with a recounting of your positive qualities and accomplishments.

+ Grieve. Release unexpressed hurt, anger, and abandonment. Then soothe the Inner Child's past feelings of hopelessness and helplessness. Turn anger into self-protection and self-compassion. It may help to purchase a doll and speak your feelings to her.

+ Cultivate safe relationships and seek support. Don't allow shame to isolate you. Educate those close to you about your flashbacks and ask them to help you work through them.

+ Learn to identify your triggers and practice preventative maintenance and trigger management.

+ Explore what it is you're flashing back to. Flashbacks point to unmet developmental needs.

+ Be patient with the recovery process; it takes time to decrease the frequency, intensity, and duration of flashbacks. Recovery is a gradual and progressive process.[22]

Dissociation

Trauma generates another common response. When a disruption in the normal psychological function of the conscious mind occurs, allowing the mind to separate itself from experiences that are too overwhelming for the psyche to process, this is known as *splitting off* or *dissociation*.[23]

High levels of dissociative symptoms are found in adult survivors whose child abuse was particularly violent or gruesome. The abuse was too much to bear, and since the child was physically unable to leave during the sexual assault, she left psychologically. This mental escape allowed her to split away from her present, painful circumstance by cutting off inner thought and awareness of what was going on. Instead, she dissociated and traveled somewhere else that was pleasant and soothing in her mind.

Children who dissociate unconsciously separate themselves from pain by storing memories in another room in their mind—in a place that becomes unavailable to the conscious mind. They mentally and emotionally "check out." This is a powerful survival skill, and the survivor learns that it's an effective, though temporary, way of escaping sexual abuse.

But an acceptable and useful childhood coping skill loses its effectiveness for an adult. Dissociation teaches a child that when a situation becomes intense or emotionally overwhelming she can split from reality and "numb out." Dissociation often occurs automatically, even when it isn't necessary or desired. Splitting no longer serves a positive function when it prevents a woman from being "present."

If you're experiencing unwanted dissociation, or if you suspect that you're often dissociating, find professional help. Your healing journey should include learning how to stay in the present and grounded in reality.

The following tips can help you check back in after you check out and dissociate:

+ Take a deep breath and ask yourself, Where am I?
+ Identify objects in the room.
+ Calculate simple math problems.
+ Use your phone.

    a.   Set your background image to something soothing, and focus on that image. For instance, my cell phone wallpaper features fish swimming through a beautiful underwater seascape.

    b.   Read through recent texts to orient yourself to time and space.

    c.   Record your emotional state and your triggers.

◆ Practice!

The Circumstances Surrounding Your Childhood Abuse

Our stories are unique, and each of us has responded distinctively to our abuse. You're the one who gets to determine the ways in which you've been scarred. But several factors contribute to the degree of impact the abuse has left on you. We live in a "both/and" and not in an "either/or" world. While many of the topics below may apply directly to you, others may not. Keep in mind, too, that while the act of abuse might have been similar for multiple survivors, the wound may be different.

Your Relationship to the Abuser

Generally, sexual abuse committed by a stranger does less emotional damage than the same kind and degree of abuse perpetrated by a parent or other close, trusted authority figure. Because a trust bond has been established between the child and someone she knows, she suffers more profoundly when that trust is violated; the aftermath is also much more devastating and complex. In addition to the humiliation suffered because of the abuse itself, the emotional and mental ramifications of the physical event(s) are multiplied exponentially; feelings of confusion, betrayal, fear, anger, and shame are intensified—compounded by the nature of the relationship with the abuser.

Duration and Frequency of Your Abuse

As a rule, the longer the abuse continued the more negative the effect upon the child. I learned coping skills to survive my repeated abuse. Most survivors develop strategies to handle the dysfunction of their lives—perhaps not wisely or well—but strategies that work nonetheless.

The longer the abuse continues the higher the degree to which victims come to rely on defense systems to survive. This makes recovery from sustained abuse all the more difficult. Acquired behaviors—appropriate and needed in order to survive child abuse—are usually no longer needed or are unsuitable in adult life. The problem is that those behaviors have become deeply ingrained. Coping skills—as distorted and awkward as they may be—often become second nature.

Be patient with yourself if you revert to a survival skill you developed in childhood. It takes time and a sense of security to lay down those tried-and-true early weapons of survival and experiment with new ways of living. Recognize your regression to old coping skills, and remind yourself that you're no longer in danger, alone, or helpless. Lay down your weapons of defense and bask in the knowledge that you're safe.

If You Lived in the Home Where Abuse Occurred

If you lived in the same home as your abuser, you functioned in a continual state of "vigilant stress." This adds a layer of complication to your healing in that you need to learn to feel safe in your own bed. As a victimized child you couldn't let down your defenses or be caught off guard because your surroundings were too dangerous and threatening; you learned to stay alert and prepared. Still today your startle response may be acute, signaling that you're ready at the slightest inkling of danger for fight or flight. Some survivors have even been known to throw a punch when they're taken by surprise. The startle response is another symptom of abuse.

Being easily frightened or jumpy isn't the core issue. Extreme stress and vigilance may have become a way of life. Because I never knew when my bedroom door would open and more abuse would invade what should have been the sanctity of my room, and even of my bed, I remained vigilant—sleeping with one eye open. After a time, and long after the abuse had ended, I crashed under the intensity of the still unremitting stress, suffering from panic attacks and depression. Many survivors have similar responses as their bodies' way of saying they can't maintain this degree of fight-or-flight preparedness any longer.

If Your Abuser Was a Woman.

The effects of abuse at the hands of a woman are sometimes more devastating than when the abuse was perpetrated by a man. The abuse of a mother toward her child defies everything we are taught to believe about maternal instinct. We see mothers as heroines, ready at all times to protect their children from harm and danger, even to the point of laying down their lives for them. Although evidence to the contrary shatters our ideology about mothers, we know that some mothers do sexually abuse their children, a reality that often remains unexamined. Both mother-son incest and mother-daughter incest exist, and the associated acts are among the most devastating of all sexual abuse encounters, as well as among the most difficult from which to recover.

For several years I facilitated support groups for sexual abuse survivors seeking healing and recovery under the acronym OASIS, standing for Overcoming and Surviving in Strength. I recall one group in particular. One member, whom I'll call Rhonda, struggled to participate. Each week while the other participants expressed grief over abuse from fathers, brothers, and uncles, she sat quietly, except for an occasional shifting in her chair.

One night we were exploring the deep shame we all felt connected to our abuse. Rhonda broke down completely, her unexpected cries riveting the attention of the startled women.

"How could my own *mother* sexually abuse me? You think *you're* bad? I must be *really* bad."

Rhonda's words sliced through the air before trailing off into soft, heartbroken sobs.

None of us had ever envisioned this scenario; we were ignorant—unaware that a mother would sexually abuse her own daughter. Even in our efforts to extend help to her, Rhonda felt alienated. She reasoned that if mothers are instinctively wired to love and nurture their children, there must have been something really monstrous about the child whose mother exploited her in this way.

It makes sense that Rhonda would have interpreted her circumstances this way, especially in a world that's loaded with contrary myths about mothers and their natures and roles. It was easier for her to believe that the abuse was her fault than to admit that the person who was supposed to love and protect her had instead so flagrantly harmed her.

If a woman has abused you—whether it was your mother, your grandmother, your aunt, or another respected figured—you'll want to take special care in addressing this. You have probably questioned your own maternal instincts; alarmingly, researchers estimate that one-third of abused and neglected children do grow up to abuse their own children when they become parents.[24]

Don't allow fear to torment you. Instead, bring your concerns into the light, opening the door to healing and resolution.

The Type of Abuse You've Endured

Regardless of the nature of your sexual abuse, you endured a brutal invasion. Your will was overruled, your voice silenced, and your body ravaged. Yet we falsely believe that the "degree" of abuse determines the severity of its impact on us. "It is often assumed that touching and fondling of the breasts and genital area is less traumatic than vaginal or rectal penetration, or oral sex. Not only is this assumption untrue, but other forms of non-touching sexual abuse can be equally devastating from the child's point of view."[25]

Connie, a woman I met while I was an associate pastor at a large church, never experienced penetration when she was abused by her father. But his tactics were no less abusive and her pain no less traumatic. "My stomach churned when the final school bell rang. On days he wasn't standing at the corner, I skipped all the way home. But when I saw him waiting for me, I was nauseous and light-headed. I knew we were 'going for a ride.'" Connie endured sporadic sexual molestation from her father, but she agonized daily from physical symptoms of stress and anxiety. Today she suffers from acute panic attacks and post-traumatic stress disorder.

Coercion and manipulation, mind-games and threats from the abuser produce profound and life-long complications. Violent, forceful acts, as well as verbal and physical abuse in combination with sexual abuse, usually intensify the damaging effects. If objects were used or the sexual abuse was physically painful and torturous, recovery is usually also more difficult.

But not impossible. Your healing is not only possible but is already in process!

Your Age at the Time of Abuse

If you were a toddler at the time of the abuse, you had less understanding of sexuality and would generally experience a reduced traumatic aftermath. You were too young to realize that this kind of "touching" was wrong. If you were unaware at the time that a crime was being committed against you, the shame and guilt associated with abuse have probably not been as prevalent as they might otherwise have become. If you were old enough to possess some degree of sexual awareness, you were more likely to have been psychologically scarred.[26]

The Response You Received
If You Told about Your Abuse

Many children don't tell anyone about their abuse for a variety of reasons. In fact, most survivors have intense fear about telling someone they've been abused.

What if I get in trouble?
If I tell, everyone will hate me.
What if no one believes me?

These fears often stem from lies abusers have used to silence the child. She has quite possibly also been weighed down with threats from her abuser, like "If you tell anyone what you've done, something awful will happen to you and your family." She may also have developed a special bond with her abuser. Although she wants the abuse to stop, she doesn't want him or her to get into trouble.

But once a survivor does tell about her abuse, the response she receives from others is of utmost importance. If a significant person believes and supports her, their acceptance helps minimize the negative spiritual and psychological effects. Experts state that a compassionate and supportive response is the most important factor in preventing sexual abuse from destroying a child's life. If a survivor reports her sexual abuse, however, and is in response blamed, ridiculed, disbelieved, or—worst of all—ignored, she's wounded all over again. She's often more ravaged emotionally by the sting of that rejection, in fact, than she was by the sexual assault.

If Your Abuse Was Incest

Sexual activity that takes place between family members is known as incest. Incest is taboo in almost all cultures—a shameful and despicable sexual assault committed against a member of a person's own family. Of the sexual incest incidents reported, more cases are cited in stepfamilies than in biological families.

From fondling to intercourse, incest is the most common form of sexual abuse perpetrated against children, yet most incest survivors I've met admit that they didn't report their abuse at the time it was occurring. Incest goes unreported for many reasons:

+ The abuse survivor cares about the abuser and is afraid of what will happen to him or her if she tells.
+ The abuse survivor is told that the activity is "normal in families" and that everyone else's family does the same thing. The child may not realize she is being abused.
+ The abuse survivor is too young to seek help outside the family.
+ The abuser has threatened the child.

Most often the child is deeply connected to the family or to the family member and is told that if she tells anyone she will ruin the family. Survivors get the message that "if family harmony is disrupted, it will be your fault." I believed my father's threat for a long time: "If you tell your mother, she'll fall apart."

Other effective lies that abusers use to silence children include

+ "You're special, and this is our special secret."
+ "Telling will kill your mother/father."
+ "I'll have to leave you, and no one will ever see me again."
+ "No one will like you or ever talk to you again."
+ "This is my way of showing you how much I love you. Not everyone gets this kind of attention from me."
+ "I'm preparing you to handle those teenage boys who are sniffing around you."
+ "I'm the parent, and you have to obey me."

Because they're threatened and manipulated, children are left, alone and confused, to deal with their secret. While the sexual wounding per se is immense, incest adds profound and often permanent psychological injury. One reason for this deep psychological scar is the intense and intermingled—though often ambivalent—emotional bond children share with their abusers. It isn't uncommon for children to love and hate their abusers at the same time.

I loved and wanted the acceptance and attention of my father, but I hated him for the way he gave it. I'm not alone.

Most survivors are abused by someone they know, so a loving and trusting relationship often existed between the child and her abuser before the abuse. Abusers take advantage of children's affections, and some go to great lengths to nurture and strengthen a trusting relationship before they molest the child. This is called "grooming" and is an attempt to prepare the child for intended abuse. When children are abused by someone they love, massive emotional conflict results.

If One or Both Parents Were
Substance Abusers or Violent

Children reared in homes in which they're exposed to substance abuse or domestic violence experience a higher rate of abuse than children from families in which these behaviors aren't present. Substance abuse and addiction cause impairment and often contribute to violence. Children in homes where violence occurs are physically abused or neglected at a rate 1500% higher than the national average.[27] Such children are placed at risk in several ways.

Intoxicated parents lose their inhibitions and release their sexually abusive behaviors under the influence of substances. I rationalized the sexual molestation from my father by blaming his alcoholism.

Substance-abusing parents neglect their children and fail to protect them from abusive siblings, other family members, or other potentially dangerous situations.

Appropriate roles and boundaries for family members become blurred. Parental inversion results—the child "parents" the adult, making decisions and caretaking on behalf of the father and/or mother. Because the spouse of an addicted parent is often left with unmet personal needs, children are expected to fill the vacancies. It isn't unusual for children to assume duties such as cooking, caring for younger siblings, and housecleaning. Eventually, the leap to taking "care" of a parent's sexual need is made—and sadly, justified by the abusing parent.

You have your own story, and the unique circumstances surrounding your abuse experience have contributed to shape you. The more you know about the details of your past, the better prepared you'll be to understand yourself and find healing.

CLOSING UP SHOP

Fearing Closeness and Intimacy

I want to be loved—not fondled, poked, pushed, squeezed, rubbed, pulled, stroked, thrust, or bent. Can you please hug me? Caress my soul, not my body. —DELORIS

Damaged Goods? Me?

My husband's words stung me like the snap of a wet rag: "What do you know about anything?"

I shot back, "Why don't you learn? I told you I don't like when you touch me there." I threw off the blankets, leaped out of bed, and stomped from the bedroom. But not before I heard his muffled retort: "You don't like me to touch you anywhere. You're a porcupine."

Admitting that I was sexually frozen was both humiliating and painful. So I blamed my husband.

I understood that our problem stemmed from my hang-ups, but I didn't know why I'd become sexually as cold as ice.

What's happening to me? I cried to myself week after week.

In those early days of my first marriage I was unaware that I had a sexual problem that stemmed from my abuse.

The first few months of my marriage to Terry had been laced with numerous hot and steamy romantic interludes. Sexual intimacy flowed naturally, with gentle ease and freedom. But soon a distaste for sex surfaced from within my broken soul, and Terry and I became unsuspecting victims. I had no idea that I'd been deeply injured or that scars from my abuse would all but kill my sex life with my eager young husband.

A wounded part of me was cowering in the shadows, terrified, as Terry tried to draw close to me. Today, in retrospect, I understand that my "child within" was paralyzed with fear, frozen by the trauma of sexual assault. To her the experience of being touched, let alone being approached for sex, was terrifying. As I discovered more about my broken self, I learned that I held many negative attitudes and beliefs about sex. I hated sexuality based on my knowledge that its lust hurt people. I hated the male sex drive because I thought of it as selfish and barbaric. I hated the sexual encounter because I believed the expectations for me to be demanding and demeaning. And I was angry because my husband expected sex to be an important component of our marriage and found it hard to show his love for me outside that context.

It wasn't that I didn't realize how distorted my feelings were, but until healing was initiated those feelings just *were*. Right or wrong, this was how I felt and the substance of what I believed.

Survivors and Sex

Many survivors of sexual abuse struggle to experience an enjoyable and positive sex life. In many cases the awakening of their sexuality and their first exposure to sexual acts happened during abuse. As a result sex became indelibly linked in their memory with abuse—making what should have been mutually pleasurable for themselves and their adult partner a painful, shameful, and utterly confusing experience for them—not to mention frustrating and equally confusing for their unsuspecting spouse.

Not only do abuse survivors view sex through a distorted lens, but the human brain also makes an association: **sex equals unpleasant and distasteful.** Many survivors involuntarily experience negative feelings—both emotionally and physically—at the very thought of sex and sexual encounters.

Our brains are designed to protect us from pain. If I touch a hot stove and get burned, I learn quickly to avoid the stove. I may even develop a fear of hot things. As survivors, we believe that sex has hurt us. In an attempt to protect us from further pain, our brain decides to avoid all things sexual. We develop an unconscious resistance to or fear of sex. Who wants to relive awful moments when we felt trapped, debilitated, violated, lost, confused, and frightened?

Why would we voluntarily place ourselves in situations that caused us to feel panicked, threatened, hyper-vigilant, ashamed, dirty, or naughty? So we learned to shut down. After all, "being sexual" had caused us untold harm, right?

Wasn't it better to deny that part of our being, to board up the door of our sexuality and close up shop?

More Abuse Fallout

The aftermath of abuse also strikes as we discover that another piece of ourselves has been destroyed: our sexuality itself.

God created us with a vast capacity for intimacy and sexuality. That beautiful capacity, however, is stolen from us through sexual abuse, which maligns God's intention and design of sexual intimacy for us.

Unfortunately, many people view sexuality as evil. As someone once expressed it, "We believe that God created our minds, hearts, arms, legs, eyes, ears, and noses, but then Satan came along and slapped on our genitals." As we heal we learn to take back and accept as good and wholesome what has been twisted, broken, and shattered. We take back what has been so inappropriately ripped from us.

We begin by throwing off shame and embarrassment. I understand shame and embarrassment and can assure you that, wherever you find yourself in your "sexual reality," your experience isn't surprising or uncommon. Many survivors

+ Long for intimacy but hate sex.
+ Hate intimacy but desire sex.
+ Detest both intimacy and sex.
+ Want intimacy and want sex, but don't know how to admit it.
+ Fear everything about sex, sexuality, and intimacy.
+ Experience negative emotions about sex, including anger, hate, rage, and fear.

+ Engage in a promiscuous sex life outside a covenant relationship.
+ Are frigid or shut down sexually within marriage.
+ Have multiple affairs outside marriage but are frozen when they are with their spouse.
+ Need pornography in order to become aroused.
+ Have fantasies about being raped, again in order to become aroused.
+ Can masturbate but have no desire for sexual intimacy.
+ Are frozen sexually and have no desire for either sex or intimacy.
+ Feel shame for having sexual feelings.
+ Cry during sexual encounters.
+ Experience physical pain related to sexual encounters.
+ Desires same-sex encounters.
+ Sleep around but fear intimacy.

The good news is that your attitude about sex can change. As you heal you can redefine your sexuality and learn to enjoy sex.

Redefining Sex

Many sexual assault survivors have a negative, convoluted perspective on sex. We often perceive and describe it in terms that more accurately define *sexual abuse* than a *loving act* between two people who mutually consent.

But sexual abuse is *not* sex! Yes, it may involve a biological function commonly termed "sex," but it isn't sex in the sense of the intimate act of love it was created to be. Sexual abuse is abuse.

Perhaps many of your sexual encounters have been laced with abuse. This would make sense because sexual abuse changes survivors, making them vulnerable to accepting more abuse. Abusive sexual interaction is often the only kind of sexual interaction survivors experience, so they develop the false belief that sex involves abuse. But I must once again emphasize the truth: sexual abuse isn't sex! Even if you liked the attention you received, became aroused, or experienced an orgasm, abuse is still abuse.

Your rights were stolen.

You were forced to perform.

Your comfort and enjoyment were neither honored nor even considered.

Your needs and desires were dishonored to fulfill the selfishness of your abuser.

You were silenced, coerced, and manipulated.

You were harmed, wounded, and betrayed.

These are just a few of the characteristics of sexual abuse. None of them in any way resembles the mutuality of a sexual relationship. In a mutually loving act between two consenting adults, the backdrop looks radically different because in a loving sexual relationship

You have rights, and they are important to your partner.

Sexual participation is mutual and by consent.

Your comfort and enjoyment are considered.

Your partner offers a selfless act of love.

Your voice is welcomed and your desires honored.

You're fulfilled, satisfied, and loved.

Sex as God created and intended it is enjoyable. It took me many years to come to the point of acknowledging and experiencing that, but I've discovered it to be true. In fact, sex can be adventurous. Sadly, if you're like me your attitude toward sex has been twisted by painful, abusive encounters. But the good news is that you can be healed to the point of discovering a new and fresh perspective and experience. The key in sexual healing is to eradicate your misplaced association between sexual abuse and sex and to create a new perception—one that is open to the exciting, the enjoyable, and the fun aspects of sexuality and sexual encounter. It won't be easy, and it won't come without profound personal inner work, but sexual healing can be yours.

A caution: don't panic and rush yourself—this kind of work usually comes toward the end of a healing journey. If you aren't ready for this, it's perfectly fine for you to skip this chapter and come back to it at a later point.

Your Sexual Self-Concept

At the core of every individual lives his or her sexual self. How you view that part of your being is your *sexual self-concept*. Survivors are often confused and disgusted by this part of their essence since they believe it to be the culprit that caused or made possible their soul-wound.

But discarding, ignoring, or shaming your sexual self is like "throwing out the baby with the bathwater," as the old saying goes. I pray that you don't discard your sexual self because you falsely connect it to your sexual abuse. That part of you is crying out to be discovered, liberated, and healed.

Common misconceptions about sexuality include the following distortions:

+ **I have to be sexual in order to be loved.** Therefore, I act sexually inappropriate to gain attention.
+ **It's better for me to be asexual.** Sex hurts people I love.
+ **My sexual self is dirty and disgusting.** Therefore, I hide her, allowing her only to act out in private.
+ **My sexual self is separate from my emotional, spiritual, intellectual, and physical self.** I scold her for her desires and keep her needs suppressed.
+ **I am completely confused by my sexuality.** I will never be able to be "normal."
+ **I'm afraid of my sexual self.** If I let her out, she'll become out of control and promiscuous.

Roadside Check-up

1. Attempt to identify where you are in each of the three areas we have explored:
    + Your present beliefs and outlook
    + Your core attitude
    + Your sexual self concept

2. Write down a statement about yourself in each of the three above areas.

3. Are you satisfied and fulfilled with where you find yourself? Why or why not?

4. Write down where you would like to be in each area. What would have to happen for you to move from your current condition to that alternate place you would like to be?

5. Pray, either in your own words or using this formulation: "Jesus, you made me. You see me. Please show me the way to becoming whole. I want your very best. I reclaim my sexuality for Your glory and for Your purpose. Lead me into all truth. Set me free from the lies of the enemy that are keeping me bound. Heal my mind, my soul, and my sexuality, Amen."

◆　◆　◆

The Sexual Healing Journey

The healing steps survivors have to take to reclaim their sexuality, healthy sexual intimacy, and loving sex can often bring them face-to-face with their greatest fears. As you travel the healing path, you may encounter the following roadblocks and detours.

Confusion about Your Sexual Rights

A stranger breaks into someone's house. The family is violated. The culprit has stolen the family's right to feel safe in their own home.

A harassing kid bullies another child on the playground, steals his lunch, and eats it. The bully has stolen the other students' right to an education free from fear.

A male boss swats a female employee on the butt, then offers her a promotion. Her boss has violated her right to a respectful work environment in which she isn't sexually harassed.

Someone overpowered you and injured you sexually. Beyond molesting your body, they raped your mind and soul. The perpetrator stole your sexual rights and left you wounded. But you still have rights! You have the right

to formulate your own opinion about sex.

to be free from coercion and manipulation.

to control when and how others touch you.

to enjoy a free and full sex life.

to be a sexual person and to grow in your sexuality.

to feel safe during sex.

to enjoy a healthy sex life.

to naturally develop in your sexuality.

to determine whether or not you will be touched.

to say no.

Accepting Touch

So how *can* you learn to become comfortable with sexual intimacy? You can begin by exploring your attitude and feelings about touch.

Some women place a moratorium on sex as they work through their sexual healing. This can be a positive step if you are actively working toward sexual recovery, allowing you the opportunity to explore your thoughts and feelings about sex, touch, and intimacy. You can begin by learning to experience and enjoy non-sexual touch.

Create new associations. Replace feelings of coercion, obligation, and guilt with connections involving comfort, soothing and pleasurable touch, and physical and emotional enjoyment.

Sexual healing is a time to identify and redirect negative thought patterns about sex and your sexuality. Give yourself permission to become a sexual person, to feel arousal and desire.

Sexual healing includes addressing your dislikes, fears, and concerns about sexual intimacy. What specific aspects turn you off or cause you to shut down? What might help you become comfortable and open up?

One young wife—I'll call her Raquel—shared that she and her husband, Mark, had yet to have sexual intercourse even though they had been married for several months. "Every time we try to have sex my vagina spasms and shoots pain up and down my legs." After months of bitter tears, mounting frustrations, and painful attempts to follow through with sex, Mark and Raquel sought medical help. Surprisingly, they discovered that Raquel was suffering from *vaginismus*, a painful spasmodic contraction of the vagina in response to physical touch or pressure. Once they medically addressed Raquel's problem, as well as her associated fears, Mark and Raquel went on to grow in their sexual relationship. Although it wasn't easy, both were committed to reclaiming a healthy sex life. Today they are experiencing freedom and wholeness.

Comfort in Intimacy

Intimacy goes beyond having sex. Some survivors feel ambivalent about using their body to sexually satisfy a partner, and that same person, when invited to participate in intimacy, freezes with fear.

Intimacy is emotionally deep.

A phrase often used to describe intimacy is *"in to me see."* Intimacy requires a trusted intertwining of yourself with another in self-revealing, positive engagement, along with a shared vulnerability and understanding. At its very core intimacy involves two selves mutually *knowing* and being *known*.

This depth of closeness, however, can leave us feeling exposed, vulnerable, . . . and frightened. In the mind of a survivor, vulnerability equates to hurt. Our culture defines vulnerability as weak, susceptible, powerless, defenseless, and helpless. And there's an element of truth in those synonyms—vulnerability makes us susceptible to hurt because it forces us to let down our shields.

But I'd like to challenge your perspective on vulnerability. Think of vulnerability as being *powerful*. In allowing yourself to engage in selective and chosen vulnerability, *you* exercise control. You freely give yourself away. You aren't being victimized or overpowered. You're *allowing* yourself to be close, to be touched, releasing yourself into the trusting arms of the one you love. Your active decision to engage in intimacy *empowers* you.

Survivors rarely transition from fear of closeness to complete surrender in intimacy. A connection like that requires the love of a patient and trusted spouse, and not every woman has that gift in equal measure. But on the healing path to sexually recovery, comfort in intimacy is key to regaining sexual fulfillment and satisfaction. Steps can be taken toward physical closeness and intimacy. You can learn to slip out of your emotional and psychological protective armor and to lovingly yield to your partner. For more on this, see Appendix 9.

Little or No Desire

Sexual interest involves more than hormones, including also psychological, spiritual, and physiological components.

For women with an abuse background, sexual desires become twisted and confusing, so that it's easier for them to cope if they emotionally escape. During sexual abuse survivors learn to turn off their sexual feelings. Their suffering is intense, so they divert their thoughts through deliberate distraction. Many women prefer to remain numb and disconnected. Because of painful associations, survivors learn to suppress their sexual desires and even to hate their bodies for having carnal urges. When they receive signals from their body that say *I want to be sexual*, they react with disgust and abhorrence. They avoid sex and situations that could potentially lead to sexual encounters.

When I was single I wanted a great sex life. But once I married I discovered that I was so deeply wounded I wanted nothing to do with sex. I desired physical touch and closeness, but when I faced the reality of sexual touch I became flooded with feelings, memories, and unwanted sensations, all reminding me of a past I'd worked hard to bury. I refused to allow myself to be a sexual being or to develop sexual desire.

Learning to accept and appreciate yourself as a sexual being is a positive step toward developing a healthy sex drive.

Issues with Trust

It is often very scary to be vulnerable, to trust and to love when you've learned about these behaviors as a child makes avoidance seem a reasonable and sane reaction. If you don't do this hard work, then your childhood was lost (not in

your control). Now you've virtually decided to become your own abuser, robbing yourself of a peaceful, joyful, fulfilling, challenging, exciting life (in your control).
—DR. LAURA SCHLESSINGER

Betrayal and abuse lurk at the core of a survivor's trust issues. Someone they loved and trusted assaulted them, and this eroded their ability to believe and have confidence in the integrity, goodness, character, safety, and honesty of others. The incest survivor cries, "Someone I loved and trusted violated me. I will never trust again." Yet without trust, deep and intimate relationships can't be achieved.

As you learn to open up in intimacy, trust also develops. Learning to trust yourself is the best place to start. Do you trust your instincts? Your decisions? Your choices? The basis for trusting others will flow from your ability to trust yourself. If you can learn to do that, you can move on to trusting your spouse. You've made a wise choice.

As you learn to trust, evaluate these elements with regard both to yourself and to your partner:

+ Are we respectful and considerate of each other?
+ Are we open and honest?
+ Are we reliable and consistent?
+ Are we confidential and faithful?

Triggers During Sex

I want a sex life where I'm grounded and present, not hurled into the past, fighting off ghosts. —A SURVIVOR

Susceptibility to triggers isn't uncommon for abuse survivors. Battles with unwanted and intrusive memories, flashbacks, panic reactions, and disorientation while engaging in sexual activity can crash in on you like a demanding toddler. These automatic responses come hard and fast, and usually without warning. Learn to identify your triggers and to link them with past negative sexual encounters; this will help you better understand how your past is influencing your present. Talk about your triggers with your partner. This will help you avoid internalizing your fears or disassociating in order to escape.

Common triggers include smells, such as cologne, toothpaste, gum, body odor, or alcohol; as well as sounds, like breathing, bed noises, music, and footsteps. Other triggers can be words the abuser used, such as "relax," or being touched in certain places on your body. These are just a few of the many sensations that can trigger negative visceral reactions.

The sexual healing journey is a long process punctuated by ups and downs, joys and sorrows, victories and defeats. Despite the arduous road, however, reclaiming your sexuality and your sex life is an important and fulfilling part of your recovery. This chapter is intended to be a catalyst to healing and not a comprehensive guide, but the journey it introduces will breathe powerful new life into your soul and your relationships.

— *Part 3* —

DISCERNING THE TRUTH

Exposing Post-Trauma Lies and Distortions

FLIPPING THE SCRIPT OF DISTORTIONS
Rejecting Lies and Rehearsing Truth

Sometimes monsters are invisible, and sometimes demons attack you from the inside. Just because you cannot see the claws and the teeth does not mean they aren't ripping through me. Pain does not need to be seen to be felt. —EMM ROY, THE FIRST STEP

The Monster

A monster lurked inside my soul, blinding me from seeing the truth.

He whispered lies and twisted tales until he bound me in his deception and distortions. I didn't know who I was, or whether anyone loved me. I certainly didn't love myself.

Then Jesus came. He spoke to my hurting inner child and to my detached, ambivalent adult self. His voice of authority slayed the monster, and through His Word He revealed the Truth to me.

This is how the gift of freedom came into my life.

No magic pill dispelled the pain, but my experience was supernatural. Through counseling and the help of the Holy Spirit, I began to recognize lies that had long festered, unexposed to truth. Still today I sometimes hear obsolete inner narratives echoing in my soul. When I ask God to help me, though, he still shines His light and expels the darkness. He helps me refute every lie and to replace it with truth.

I tell prisoners, 'Come on out. You're free!' and those huddled in fear, 'It's all right. It's safe now.' —THE PRE-INCARNATE JESUS IN ISAIAH 49:9, MSG

The Monster of Deception

We were children when the monster appeared, uninvited, into our lives. Our young minds were incapable of comprehending the abuse. We endured what we lacked the capacity to understand, but to make sense of it all our brain conjured up "stories"—inner narratives about *why* our abused was happening.

As we grew and learned about the world, these early interpretations protected us and saved us from emotional and mental implosion. But the conclusions and stories we had created about our trauma—whether conscious or subconscious—functioned like a GPS (Global Positioning System), guiding and dictating the course of our lives. Many of us were driven to act upon what we believed—"I'm dirty—it's all my fault." But once those false stories were no longer needed for our survival—or helpful for our functioning—we discovered that they'd taken on a life of their own.

A monster comprised of distorted thoughts combined with Satan's lies had overtaken our thoughts, ripping us apart from the inside and perpetuating our abuse.

For healing to flow in your life, you must confront the monster within. That means traveling back through your past and re-interpreting your trauma through the lens of maturity, truth, knowledge, and healing—speaking comfort and love to the helpless, powerless, wounded child within you as an empowered woman with God by your side.

Shelly Beach, co-founder of PTSDPerspectives.org and co-author of *Love Letters from the Edge: Meditations for Those Suffering from Brokenness, Trauma, and the Pain of Life*, says

> Unfortunately, those who experience trauma often don't understand that the deeply painful experiences that overwhelm us produce biological and chemical consequences as well as spiritual and emotional consequences. Body chemistry does not end at the neck, and the same chemicals that influence the liver, kidneys, and heart also influence cells and blood vessels in the brain. Expect trauma recovery to be hard work but some

of the most valuable work you will ever do. God is with you and for you on this journey of defeating self-destructive, ineffective coping patterns.[28]

As an abuse survivor I believed my share of distortions and falsehoods. You've probably identified some lies already. Is it time now for you to go back and process your past through the lens of Truth? Until you do, false beliefs and distortions will influence your daily life and choices and continue to hold you captive.

Roadside Check-up

Think about your story. Pay attention to "internal interpretations" of why the abuse happened to you. Internal interpretations are viewpoints that focus on *you* as the center of the blame. For example, "I was abused because I was acting naughty that day." Reframe your story using only external interpretations, viewpoints that substitute outside factors as the source of the trauma. What do you discover? Be sure to write down your insights.

Lies We Believe

"How do I know if I'm believing a lie?" Rachael asked me.

"Would you be willing to share some of your story with me? Why do you think sexual abuse happened to *you*, and how do you feel the abuse affected you?"

Rachael eagerly shared her story. "I guess it happened to me because I was the most like my mom. Dad told me I had the devil in my eyes just like she did and he had to purge me from that evil. But that was a long time ago. I've grown a lot since then, and I'm pretty much over it."

As Rachael and I talked about her experience, we discovered that she held to several false beliefs:

+ Identification with her mother was bad. So she rejected her mother and hated parts of herself that were like her mom.
+ God didn't love her because she was like the devil. She felt unworthy of God's love, and when bad things happened she surmised that God was punishing her.
+ Because the abuse was over and no longer affected her, she had no need to seek help. Her denial kept her locked in destructive patterns of self-harm, addiction, and other numbing behaviors.

False beliefs and distorted stories twist like choking vines around the minds of sexual assault survivors. A child's vulnerable mind offers the ideal setting for Satan to spin misconceptions and weave them into our psyche. Our immature, faulty reasoning accepts those lies, and our mind weaves together a belief system of which we are often unaware.

The survivor's filter of lies becomes powerful and destructive. After a time we progress from *thinking* that our false beliefs are true to unconsciously working to "prove" them true because our brains seek continuity. Science tells us that our brains gather evidence to support what we already believe. If I believe that "no one loves me," for example, my brain will be on the alert for confirmation of that premise. I will either imagine my own rejection or act in ways that will cause me to be rejected.

Unless survivors intentionally work to unearth and dismantle their lies, they will live like victims, controlled and manipulated by distorted stories. This step was a critical part of my journey, and I hope it will be part of yours, too.

A number of factors influence how deeply and how pervasively false beliefs control your life: the type of abuse you've encountered, the duration of your abuse, and your relationship to the person who abused you. According to certified trauma specialist Candace Johnson, LMSW, ACSW, CTS, "Stage(s) of development at the time of abuse and amount exposure to abuser are factors in the impact of the lie. Attachment to the abuser is another factor."[29] Determine whether any of the following distorted thoughts or beliefs are influencing your life:

The Lie: It was my fault.

The Consequence: We experience false guilt and shame.

This lie is a big one.

Kids rely on magical thinking—they believe that everything has to do with them and often see themselves as the cause of negative circumstances. This is often seen when children's parents divorce. "It's my fault my mommy and daddy aren't together anymore," they think.

The same holds true with sexual abuse. Children believe "It's my fault" and "I did something to deserve it." Variations include

+ I should never have trusted him or her.
+ I should have told someone.
+ I should never have worn that dress.
+ I was needy. I shouldn't have wanted love.
+ I was stupid and naive.
+ I should have said no.

As survivors, we blame ourselves and take responsibility. This is a classic survival technique. After all, if it was my fault I can stop it from ever happening again. I have power over it.

We blame ourselves and rehearse ways in which we should have fought off or refused to participate in our abuse. We heap shame and guilt upon ourselves: "I'm responsible. I should have . . ."

It's important to understand that passivity isn't consent and that it's by far the most common reaction to childhood sexual abuse. The frontal lobe of our brain; the control center where decisions are made, becomes frozen paralyzing us until abuse is over.

At a recent women's conference at which I spoke a woman named Dorothy got up from her seat and walked to the front to receive prayer. As she came forward, God spoke to my heart: "Tell her it wasn't her fault." I was taken aback at how clearly the words came to me. I knew I had to give her the message, but I still worried: *What if I heard wrong? She'll think I'm crazy.*

But the message was too clear for me to dismiss.

As we joined hands to pray, I leaned toward the woman's ear and whispered, "This may seem strange to you, but I believe God gave me a message for you. He wants you to know, 'It's not your fault.'"

Dorothy doubled over, as though she'd been punched in the stomach, and let out a cry. As she sobbed uncontrollably, I knelt beside her and asked, "What can I do for you?"

"You have no idea what this means to me. I've carried the guilt of my childhood rape for years. Today I told God I needed to know if I was to blame. He answered my prayer." Then she shouted for all to hear, "It's not my fault! It's not my fault! It's not my fault!"

Sexual abuse is *never* the child's fault.

Never.

No matter the circumstances surrounding the experience, children are blameless. The responsibility lies solely with the abuser.

Jesus Himself made this clear: "Whoever welcomes a little child like this in my name welcomes me. But if anyone causes one of these little ones who believe in me to sin, it would be better for him to have a large millstone hung around his neck and to be drowned in the depths of the sea" (Matthew 18:5–6).

The Lie: I'm bad.

The Consequence: We experience feelings of low self-worth and esteem.

"Flawed." "Contaminated." "Defective." "Damaged goods."

Many survivors use words like these to describe themselves. Self-rejection is for them an intense, reoccurring struggle. A woman looks in the mirror and hates what she sees. She despises herself and feels as though she doesn't measure up to others. Her self-esteem was shattered long before her adult life unfolded. "That's because many victims of sexual abuse feel that they *are* their abuse," explains Shelly Beach, co-suthor of *Love Letters from the Edge*. "They feel damaged, ruined, and dirty."

An elderly woman in our support group had lived her entire life enduring feelings of self-hatred and disgust. "I can't remember a time when I felt good about myself. I've always hated me." Only when she accepted support did she begin to find self-worth.

God tells us in his Word that we've been "fearfully and wonderfully" made (Psalm 139:14). God delighted in our very creation and declared us "wonderful." Life's circumstances hurt and wounded us, but *we* aren't flawed or defective. Our identity can be renewed and restored by God's healing power.

The Lie: No one can love me. Not even God.

The Consequence: We experience rejection and abandonment.

Because of deep-seated shame and self-loathing, wounded women often settle for relationships that are toxic and dysfunctional. They frequently attract men who continue to abuse them. This confirms the lie that *No one will love me.* After a history of exploitation, this lie—coming from their abuser or from themselves—propels some survivors to accept mistreatment because they're convinced they deserve nothing better.

The truth is that women aren't commodities. Damaged self-esteem may leave them feeling as though they're nothing more than sexual objects. But women are inherently—and infinitely—valuable in the eyes of our Creator; we are anything but substandard. We are loveable.

The Lie: God can't heal me.

The Consequence: We experience victimization.

When we believe that God can't heal us, we tell ourselves that His Word and promises aren't big enough to encompass our situation. We proclaim to the world and to ourselves that we're unfixable. It goes without saying that this isn't true. God's Word is sufficient for *all* things. We aren't so unique that God is forced to make exceptions just for us. That means that God's Word is sufficient for YOU. The best news of all is that the veracity of His words doesn't depend on our fluctuating opinions, limited intellect, or unreliable emotions.

The truth is that we must accept our identity in Jesus Christ, no matter how we feel about our past actions. Then we must cling to the Word of God as the foundation for our faith as we root out the lies, renounce them, and triumphantly claim God's truth for ourselves.

The Lie: It felt good, so I must have wanted it.

The Consequence: We experience empty, false pleasure.

Survivors struggle with guilt and confusion when they experience sexual pleasure during their abuse. They feel deeply troubled and humiliated for allowing themselves to become physically stimulated. Many feel as though their bodies betrayed them in the worst way.

Most victims determine not to give their perpetrators the satisfaction of seeing them receive enjoyment during the abuse, but in spite of their rational decision physical pleasure sometimes occurs during abuse because our bodies were created to react to stimuli. Perpetrators exploit children even further when they force their victims to reach sexual fulfillment, touching their young bodies in ways intended to cause sexual arousal. Mental abuse follows when the abuser makes condemning comments, such as, "See, you enjoyed this. You really wanted it."

As a result, survivors come to hate their bodies.

But survivors need to learn to accept the truth—for themselves. When prolonged sexual stimulus occurs, a physical response sometimes takes place for sexual assault victims; their body reacts in the way it was designed, and the survivor feels pleasure. It's important to point out that this pleasure is a purely physical response, manipulated by someone more powerful than the victim. The physical reaction should never be interpreted as emotional, spiritual, or relational enjoyment.

The Lie: I have to be sexual in order to be loved.

The Consequence: We experience exploitation.

"Sex equals love."

Many survivors unconsciously believe this message. We were exploited as children, and while the attention and affection felt good, the experience was also confusing.

Who doesn't enjoy feeling loved and accepted? But we were also disgusted by the manner in which we received attention from our abusers. Unfortunately, some survivors come to the convoluted conclusion that negative attention is better than none at all.

It makes sense, then, that when survivors reach adulthood they have difficulty distinguishing between sex and love. They often believe that being loved equates to having a sexual experience. Their identity has become distorted. In the minds of survivors, sexuality and worth are synonymous.

Survivors must learn to replace their false thinking with God's truth: that we are loveable because God created us that way. We are loveable because we're His priceless creation. We are also loved because each one of us is intrinsically unique and therefore precious and special. We don't have to earn love by performing sexual acts or being sensual. We are inherently worthy of love.

The Lie: My abuse wasn't that bad. I'm over it.
The Consequence: We experience minimization.

Minimizing the impact of abuse is a classic defense mechanism for survivors. It's denial in its most damaging form. A woman in denial makes statements like:

"It hurt at the time, but I've gotten over it."

"If I act like it didn't hurt me, it didn't."

"If I ignore it, it will go away."

"I don't want to talk about it; it's buried in the past."

One woman was unfortunately told that she was violating Scripture when she complained about her hurtful past. "The Bible says you have to 'forget what lies behind.' You aren't permitted to dig it up."

Forgetting and burying the past, however, don't erase it. These tactics don't eliminate the negative symptoms that plague survivors.

Sexual abuse ripped us apart like a hurricane.

To try to live as though debris isn't scattered through our life is ridiculous. Ruin can't be swept under the rug and ignored. I know—I've tried it.

I minimized my pain and denied the enormity of the crime committed against me. I convinced myself that my abuse was *not that bad* and then discounted the negative symptoms with which I continued to struggle as being *no big deal.*

The truth is that our healing accelerates *when we admit* that we were violated, humiliated, and disgraced. We must be willing to break down our walls of denial, become vulnerable, and take an honest look at the abuse fallout scattered throughout our lives.

A survivor needs to invest time, commitment, and emotional energy in order to unearth, expose, and confront the lies and distorted messages she has come to believe. In fact, most survivors will continue to discover and address twisted beliefs throughout the remainder of their lives. But as you work through your trauma, the light of discovery will slowly seep into the dark places of your mind and illuminate your patterns of twisted thinking and controlling thoughts. You will gain freedom as you discover these distortions and replace them with God's truth.

You may notice other false narratives and stories common to abuse survivors:

+ *I can't say no.*
+ *No one listens to me.*
+ *I have nothing to offer.*
+ *I'm all alone.*
+ *I'm worthless.*
+ *I have no talents.*
+ *I can't be forgiven.*
+ *I can't trust anyone.*
+ *Everyone is out to get me.*
+ *If I want to be accepted, I have to be what people want me to be.*
+ *I must be sexual in order to receive love.*
+ *I'm responsible for everyone else's happiness.*
+ *I'm not valuable. My feelings don't matter.*
+ *Bad attention is better than no attention.*

Roadside Check-up

1. Which of the above lies, or others of your own, do you find yourself believing?

2. Challenge your thoughts and false beliefs. Ask yourself, *Is what I believe true? Why or why not?*

3. Rewrite a scenario for each false belief from a new perspective—one that is based on truth.

4. Practice telling yourself this true story whenever the "lie" whispers to you.

Flip the Script

We've discovered that false beliefs, lies, and distortions are just another ploy Satan uses to keep us victimized and bound from being the persons God created us to be. Knowing God's truth and speaking it aloud helps us to break free. So the next time those daunting fears and doubts overwhelm your soul, or those lying voices assault your spirit, flip the script! Speak God's Word over your heart and mind. Remember, what He says is TRUTH.

When . . .

I say, "I'm alone," God says, "I will never leave you."

I say, "I'm dirty," God says, "You are clean."

I say, "I'm hopeless," God says, "Hope will never disappoint you."

I say, "I'm lost and confused," God says, "I am the Way. Follow Me."

I say, "I'm broken and bruised," God says, "I am your Healer. You can trust me."

I say, "I'm afraid," God says, "My love casts out all fear."

I say, "I'm ugly," God says, "You are my treasure. You're beautiful."

I say, "I'm captive," God says, "You're free."

FINDING PEACE
Answering Difficult Questions

It's far better to be angry than numb. It means you're still asking questions. —DONNA

Questions plague survivors.

You may face doubts and questions that steal your peace. I struggled for years to find answers and find peace.

So I created a list of life-stealing questions so I could stop running from my pain and face my fears. That's when I made a powerful discovery: Truth unlocks healing.

When I honestly evaluated my questions and unchallenged answers, I realized that I'd formed "pre-set" answers rooted in shame, false guilt, and victimization. And I'd accepted these lies hook, line, and sinker.

Most survivors agree that lies are the source of our bondage.

So here's my list of "snapping dogs"—lies (voiced in the form of questions) that hound most victims of sexual abuse:

— ONE —

Was it my fault?

In the deep recesses of our souls we survivors claim culpability for our abuse. So listen up once and for all:

NO. Your abuse was NOT your fault!

Nothing you said, did, or didn't do provoked your abuse. Blame and shame for your trauma lie strictly on the shoulders of your abuser. Your abuse was their crime, their responsibility.

Period.

You may be claiming responsibility for your abuse as a way to protect yourself. You may believe that "if I caused the abuse, then somehow I have power to stop it from happening again. I'm in control." But you weren't in control of your past, and you can't control the future, either. What you can do is make a choice to free yourself from the blame, release the grudge you secretly hold against yourself for allowing yourself to be wounded, and place your trust in Jesus for each and every day that unfolds ahead of you.

Roadside Check-up

Consider the question "Was it my fault?" Then quietly listen to the true voice, Jesus, whispering His answer to your heart. Write it down.

— TWO —

Am I bad?

No. What happened to you was painful. But it doesn't make you bad. The abuser did bad things to you.

You must believe that *you* are not your abuse.

You aren't ruined, defective, "damaged goods," or wretched.

You were made in God's image and thus are beautiful.

It's possible that as a result of your abuse you've *acted out* in destructive, broken, rebellious, or other reckless ways. Acting out is a normal psychological response to abuse that is used by survivors in an attempt to reduce the anxiety and pain of trauma. In an attempt to deny and suppress the emotions and feelings associated with your trauma, you may have acted in self-destructive ways.

But YOU are valuable and worthy of love and affection. In the Bible God gives us this promise: "Do not fear, for I have redeemed you; I have summoned you by name; you are mine. When you pass through the waters, I will be with you; and when you pass through the rivers, they will not sweep over you. When you walk through the fire, you will not be burned, the flames will not set you ablaze" (Isaiah 43:1–2).

Roadside Check-up

Consider the question "Am I bad?" Then quietly listen to the true voice, Jesus, whispering His answer to your heart. Write it down.

— THREE —

Why me?

Do you ask why you were chosen to be the object of abuse? Many survivors assume that they are intrinsically flawed or defective in an attempt to explain why their sexual abuse happened. This conclusion, however, is another false form of self-protection. We rationalize that if our abuse were a result of some gross flaw within ourselves, all we have to do is "fix" ourselves. If we will only perform better, look better, work harder, and make greater achievements than others, we can spare ourselves more hurt and abuse. Thus the performance trap ensnares us. We fall prey to this snapping dog, nipping at our heels and demanding more and more perfection and performance.

The truth is that you were abused not because of something wrong about you or within you. You didn't deserve to be harmed but were the object of someone else's criminal behavior. You may have been targeted because you were timid or shy, or you may have been groomed because you were accessible. But God didn't allow your abuse because you were unloved or unlovable, or because you were a second-class human being. You were harmed because of the selfish decision of an abuser who was driven by darkness.

Roadside Check-up

Consider the question "Why Me?" Then quietly listen to the true voice, Jesus, whispering His answer to your heart. Again, write it down.

— FOUR —

Where was God?

You prayed. You cried out for God to come and rescue you. His answer? *Silence.*

It isn't uncommon for survivors to feel as though God has abandoned them. They often state, "If God is an all-powerful, supreme being, then He could have intervened and stopped the abuse. But He chose not to."

Trials generate pain and grief, and grief brings disillusionment and feelings of betrayal and anger. This feeling of betrayal—sometimes a dormant sentiment—rises up as survivors begin their healing and consider putting their faith and trust in God. There are no easy, pat answers to these questions. But finding an answer that resonates with your spirit and aligns with God's Word will release another dimension of healing for you. So ask God to speak to your heart about where He was at the time of your abuse. Here are some answers that survivors have shared with me:

+ God's heart was breaking, and He wept with me.
+ While I was being abused, God was overshadowing me, protecting me with His wings.
+ Jesus was reminding the Father of the price He paid for my healing and wholeness.
+ God was crying for me and interceding for my recovery.
+ God was writing a beautiful ending to my story.

Roadside Check-up

Consider the question "Where were you, God?" Then quietly listen to the true voice, Jesus, whispering His answer to your heart. Yet again, write it down.

— FIVE —

Why does God allow evil?

Almost everyone asks this question.

The argument that people have been created with free will seldom fully comforts survivors of trauma, but the truth of the matter is that God *has* chosen to give humanity free will in terms of their actions and reactions. If He hadn't made that choice we'd all be puppets, without the freedom to choose our own path—or even to voluntarily offer up to Him our praise and obedience.

But God loves us so much that He granted all humanity in every era of history autonomy and freedom of choice. After all, love that is coerced isn't love at all. God's inexpressible love for us necessitates that He not violate that "free will" principle.

We've been endowed with the freedom to love or reject God, to obey and walk in His will and righteousness or to disobey and commit evil acts—acts that hurt and violate others.

When someone chose to commit an evil act against you, God grieved and wept *with you* over the pain the perpetrator of that evil was inflicting on you. He didn't turn a blind eye or a deaf ear. He did see, does hear, and has planned your healing, recovery, freedom, and redemption.

God determined long before your conception that He would heal you and set you free from the atrocities that would wound you. He can, and without a doubt longs to, make you stronger than you would ever have been if you hadn't faced life's struggles. God's plan for you includes

+ Deepening your insight into His character and His Word. He gives you depth of strength and insight (Psalm 119:71).
+ Working out the ramifications of this trial for your ultimate good. You are an overcomer (Romans 8:38).
+ Giving you a testimony that will glorify Him. You are a powerful witness on His behalf (2 Corinthians 3:2; Ephesians 2:10).
+ Giving you a sensitive and caring heart for the hurts of others. You are a compassionate healer (2 Corinthians 1:3–4).

+ Using your life to encourage others. You are a trophy of grace (Isaiah 58:12).
+ Teaching you how to wait on Him and listen for His voice. You are trusted by God to function as His minister (Isaiah 40:31).
+ Instilling within you true joy that isn't based on circumstances. You wield deep spiritual influence (Habakkuk 3:16–19).

Understanding God and His ways is far beyond our human capability. But sometimes our unresolved God-issues can produce an inaccurate view of who God is and how He loves us.

As we journey through healing, we awaken to a more complete, accurate, and biblically based view of God. Descriptions of God found in His Word help us learn who He truly is. We see that He isn't just a God who *was*, but a God who *IS*. Among His many other wonderful attributes, God is:

+ Love   1 John 4:16
+ Patience   Numbers 14:18; 2 Peter 3:9
+ Kindness   Romans 2:4
+ Faithfulness   1 Corinthians 1:9; 2 Timothy 2:13
+ Compassion   Psalm 116:5
+ Justice   2 Thessalonians 1:6
+ Peace   Ephesians 2:14
+ Ever-present   Deuteronomy 31:6–8

Roadside Check-up

Consider the question "Why did God allow this evil?" Then quietly listen to the true voice, Jesus, whispering His answer to your heart. As you've done before, write it down.

— SIX —

Does God love me?

Absolutely—infinitely so! You're a treasure of magnificent worth—the priceless jewel of God's love. The Bible, in fact, constitutes God's love letter to you. He speaks of His love for you over and over again and assures you that He has a plan for your life. His endless love for you is unchallenged and unchanged by anything you can or won't do.

God's Word also assures you that He doesn't lie—ever! If you can accept that God's Word is true—infallible, unerring, and flawless—you can accept by faith that He loves you to the point of inscribing your name on the palms of His own hands—an indelible tattoo. He *can't* forget you.

However, the freedom to choose to believe rests with you. Don't rely on your feelings to confirm God's love or "prove" His care. You may not *feel* loved. But emotions are never the measure of truth. Surrender yourself to trust and faith. Let go of your doubts and fluctuating feelings.

God is safe. You can trust Him.

Roadside Check-up

Consider the question "God, do You love me?" Then quietly listen to the true voice, Jesus, whispering His answer to your heart. Write it down.

— SEVEN —

Will I ever heal?

Healing is possible for you. Yes, *you*. But healing involves a process that produces a cycle of ups and downs. So don't be surprised if you find yourself at times taking three steps forward and two steps back. This cycle may take a little longer, but it still brings progress, so don't get discouraged.

Once you choose healing and pursue wholeness, you will begin to heal. It's normal to discover that emotional scarring remains after you've processed the bulk of your trauma, but the painful, festering wound will have begun to heal, and you can ultimately enjoy a full and wonderful life, free of the aftermath of abuse. Just remember that healing is a process that will take as long as it takes.

Roadside Check-up

Consider the request "God, show me how I'm healing." Then quietly listen to the true voice, Jesus, whispering His words of assurance to your heart. Write them down.

— EIGHT —

Do I have to forgive?

Forgiveness is a choice. It's also a process. Deciding to forgive is something we can instantly do with our human will, but that doesn't mean our feelings will instantaneously change. Forgiving doesn't mean that our healing is complete or that we will no longer experience pain.

Not at all.

Forgiveness is a door we open to let out the poison. It allows the toxicity to dissipate, to find its way out of our life so that healing can take place. We repeat the choice to forgive as we incrementally remember and heal more and more. We forgive at deeper levels, releasing greater freedom in our hearts. Forgiveness happens at many stages throughout your healing process. You don't have to rush in to the process; in fact, I recommend that you don't. All too often people frustrate the flow of healing when they forgive as a form of denial, saying in effect, "I've forgiven, and now I have closure; my experience is all over." We will explore forgiveness more deeply in the chapters ahead.

Roadside Check-up

Consider the question "Have I forgiven?" Then quietly listen to the true voice, Jesus, whispering His answer to your heart. Write it down.

— NINE —

What about trust?

Whom can I trust? How do I know if I should trust? How can I trust myself? These are common questions for survivors. The undeniable truth for you as a survivor is that your capacity to trust has been diminished and that the pain of abuse has impaired your ability to feel safe. Any person in a relationship has felt, to one degree or another, the sting of broken trust. We've all been hurt, betrayed, disappointed, abandoned, and lied to. Unfortunately, imperfection is the reality of our human condition.

Since trust is an essential ingredient—if not the foundation—for life and relationships, you must learn to trust God, yourself, and others. This process begins by trusting God, the only person who will never abandon, lie to, or betray you. You must begin by believing that He will guide you and reveal Himself and His plans to you. Only then will you find the confidence to trust in yourself—in your instincts, your ability to judge character, and your discernment and wisdom. Why? Because the God and Creator of the universe has got your back!

Trusting yourself doesn't mean that you'll never make a mistake, but it does mean that no matter what happens or what challenge may come your way, you can be confident that with God at your side you can handle even the most painful situations. You aren't going to fall apart if you feel discomfort as a result of trusting once again.

Nor does trusting mean asking God or people for guarantees. Unfortunately, life doesn't come with guarantees. If you want solid promises that you'll never again be hurt or taken advantage of, you're asking for more than any imperfect human can offer. That doesn't mean the people in your life are always or necessarily untrustworthy but only that they're human. And humans will inevitably fail us and let us down. If you're waiting for others to "earn your trust" with 100% reliability, you're setting them—and ultimately yourself—up for certain failure.

Roadside Check-up

Consider the question "Can God help me trust?" Then quietly listen to the true voice, Jesus, whispering His answer to your heart. Write it down.

— TEN —

Should I confront my abuser?

There are no easy or pat answers for this question. Confronting your abuser is a decision you should make only after thoughtful consideration and counsel from wise and trusted sources. Do what feels right for you, not what someone else might have deemed "right" or "wrong" for herself. While many survivors have a desire to confront the person who wounded them, others feel healthier and safer only symbolically confronting their abuser.

If you're considering a confrontation with your perpetrator, seriously consider your answers to the following questions:

+ What would be my motive for confronting?
+ What would be my desired outcome? Is this realistic?
+ Will confrontation set me back emotionally? Am I strong enough to handle this possibility?
+ Can I live with the consequences and possible fallout of confrontation?
+ Am I willing to lose contact with those who also know the abuser?

When I confronted my abuser I was met with his denial. In that moment I felt violated all over again. Later on I discovered that perpetrators, when challenged about their crime, will almost always deny it—at least initially.

So make sure you're confronting your abuser *for yourself*, not for the response you long to receive. Abusers don't like to relinquish control, nor do they appreciate being backed into a corner, so be prepared for a belligerent reaction. Rehearse ahead of time what you plan to say. Above all, bear in mind that the confrontation is ultimately for the purpose of your own healing. You are no longer a victim, and you desire, albeit belatedly, to take control of the situation.

Roadside Check-up

Consider the question "Should I confront my abuser?" Then quietly listen as the true voice, Jesus, whispers His answer to your heart. Write it down.

— ELEVEN —

What if my abuser is dead or otherwise unavailable to me?
Can I still confront or forgive the perpetrator?

You can symbolically confront and forgive your abuser even if the individual is deceased or no longer in contact with you, or if you don't know who they are. The important thing is that God knows who they are, and offering forgiveness or finding closure through symbolic confrontation can be a powerful step in your own healing. You can write a letter you have no intention of sending, expressing how you feel and how you were hurt by their actions, or you can place an empty chair in front of you and visualize the perpetrator sitting there as you "tell" them how you feel. You can also visit the gravesite of the perpetrator and share your feelings.

Roadside Check-up

Consider the question "God, how can I release my pain?" Then quietly listen to the true voice, Jesus, whispering His answer to your heart. Write it down.

In conclusion, explanations, answers, and reasons help our hearts to find rest, but answers alone are incapable of instilling within us true peace. Explanations for our pain aren't all that we need. We need presence—the presence of the God who alone can suffuse our hearts with authentic peace. Authentic peace is transcendent peace. It goes beyond our human ability to explain "the why" and leads us to the infinitely more significant "Who." Just as God *is* love. He is also peace. Listen to the inimitable words of Paul— "And the peace of God, which transcends all understanding, will guard your hearts and minds in Christ Jesus" (Philippians 4:7)—and of the sons of Korah (psalmists)—"God is our refuge and our strength, an ever-present in help in trouble" (Psalm 46:1).

Roadside Check-up

In this moment ask God for His peace. For His serenity. And for the ability to rest in the untroubled assurance that He is working in you and for you. Open your heart to receive His peace.

SHOPPING BEYOND THE SCRATCH AND DENT SALE
Accepting Your True Value

Every woman that finally figured out her worth, has picked up her suitcases of pride and boarded a flight to freedom, which landed in the valley of change. —SHANNON L. ALDER

Our conference speaker, Lisa, held up a fifty-dollar bill. I, along with all the other women in the room, sat on the edge of my chair ready to pounce. "Who wants this fifty dollars?" she tantalized us.

I screamed and waved my hand along with all the other clamoring hopefuls.

Lisa spoke again. "Okay, I see those hands, but wait just a moment."

She crumpled the bill in her hand and wadded it up into a tight ball. "Now who wants it?"

No one's enthusiasm waned—especially mine. I cheered and waved my hand all the more.

"Okay, I see I haven't discouraged any of you. But wait—what about now?"

Lisa hurled the bill to the floor and stomped on it, ruthlessly grinding it into the ballroom floor.

"Does anyone still want it?"

"Yes!" We all cheered with delight. Our desire for the prize had not in the least been diminished.

"But why do you still want it?" Lisa probed, as though in surprise.

"Because it's worth fifty collars!" I yelled.

Lisa's illustration hit home. No matter what I'd been through in life, my value and worth hadn't been diminished. I was still a jewel of incredible worth to God. He didn't see me as damaged, soiled, or ruined. His desire for me was unchanged.

The same is true of you.

You Are Valuable

You aren't defined by your past. You no longer have to function as though you're limited. Banish the lie that tries to convince you that "living diminished keeps you safe." On the contrary, living a diminished existence puts you right in the path of oncoming destruction. Wasting away day by day is hardly playing it safe—it's dying. Quite to the contrary, *today* is your day to live—really live. It's time to emerge from the cellar into the blinding light of day, to walk into the possibilities of your life, to live out your worth, to recognize and maximize your value.

You have indeed been fearfully and wonderfully made. Your life matters—to God and to others. You deny God's purpose for you when you regard your life as though it has no value.

As I write these words I can't help but visualize the souls of untold women crumpled and trampled, just like that fifty-dollar bill. Perhaps this describes you. You feel as though the best you can do is exist. But this healing journey is about becoming courageous. *You can choose* to open your heart to God's love—and to loving yourself. You can do this by an act of will, trusting that the confirming emotions and evidence will follow. This is the essence of faith.

Until you choose to bless, love, and nurture yourself, you'll never be able to trust someone else to love you for who you are.

Start by believing God—that you are who He says you are. You're the apple of His eye, the cherished daughter on whom He dotes, the Creator of the universe—including you. Think about that for a moment. Let the magnitude of that truth dawn on you.

Then trust His love for you enough to follow His lead in loving yourself.

Damaged Goods and Other Lies

Too often we focus on who or what we believe we *are not* instead of on who and what God says we *are*.

You were wounded. Your being was assaulted. But your intrinsic value and beauty remain unchanged because they're rooted in God. They find their source in Him, not in your own or in anyone else's actions toward you. God wills it that you *can't* be "less than" anyone else. And no matter what your circumstances (your "past"), you're just as precious and worthy today as you were the moment God created you.

One of the most life-changing truths we can ever grasp is that our value is anchored in God's character and not in our circumstances, successes, or failures. This is possible because Jesus took our sin debt upon Himself so that we, in exchange, could receive the fullness of the gift of God's image in us.

Deloris often writes to me. Her childhood sexual abuse was horrific. "Three or four times a week I was assaulted by my father," she ruefully reported. "He never loved me or saw anything good in me. All he did was use me and throw me away. I'm garbage to him. I think that's how God sees me too—a worthless person, just taking up space." Still, Deloris longs to experience love and find meaning. "I've separated myself from the human race," she lamented. "No one cares for me. My hope—if I have any—is that someday, someone will come into my life and save me, love me, talk to me, and heal me on the inside. I am so damaged. But who would ever love a worthless piece like me?"

Abuse, neglect, and abandonment have conspired together to erode Deloris's self-esteem. Still today, emotional wounds tell her that she is unloved, unworthy, and unclean. She can't believe that love is possible for her. She lives devoid of joy.

Surprisingly, Deloris is an executive who earns a handsome salary, has been married for twenty years, has two children, and is a faithful churchgoer. From within the image of a perfect, "together" life, Deloris deplores, "I'm empty and so, so very damaged."

Roadside Check-up

1. Do you know how valuable and loved you are? Write down what you believe to be true in this regard and how you feel about it.

2. Do you confidently believe the realties about your value your head tells you are true? Write down what you actually believe in this regard.

3. Do you feel loved and valuable? Why or why not?

4. Compare your three answers above. Do you discover a pattern? Anything else?

5. Pray: "God, I struggle with accepting and believing that I'm as beautiful and loved as You say I am. Please drive out shame and fear by Your love and by Your Word. I choose to trust and believe that what You say about me is true—that I am loved, forgiven, worthy, and valuable beyond measure. That I am Your delight, a treasure in your eyes of magnificent worth. Today I will
   + *Accept* what you, God, say about me.
   + *Shed* the labels and the behaviors that have served as my defense mechanisms but are no longer healthy or effective for me.
   + *Embrace* my true self, come out of hiding, and be me.
   + *Speak* out loud who it is you say I am.
   Amen."

Acting Out

I don't need you to tell me I'm acting like a loser. You're already the voice in my head. —SHAWN

After abuse many young girls don't know how to express their pain. Their feelings of abandonment, mistrust, and shame often lead to lives of loneliness, withdrawal, and isolation. The paradox, however, is that the abused young woman's need for help, support, and understanding is unparalleled. When isolation doesn't alleviate her pain, she too often turns to another option: acting out.

Acting out isn't a conscious decision to behave badly and to throw off all restraint in rebellion; it's a cry—a plea for someone to "pay attention to and rescue me." Risky actions or negative behaviors are defense mechanisms, ways to cope and survive.

Unfortunately, acting out can also become the measuring stick of our value, both in our own eyes and from the perspective of others. We associate our behavior—good or bad—with our value. When we behave like a "good girl," we feel as though we deserve love, value, and worth. But when we misbehave, when we take on the role of "naughty girls," opting not to comply with the rules of good behavior, we feel as though we deserve to be unloved and devalued, that we are unworthy of the special, positive elements life would otherwise have to offer.

The following, however, is a critical truth: your behavior isn't synonymous with, nor does it determine, your value. Based on no action or influence of your own, you are deeply cherished. God esteems you and holds you in high honor, even when others fail to see your value. You are priceless—whether or not you perceive your magnificent worth.

As you walk through the steps of healing, you will learn that you no longer have to resort to bad behavior as your means of crying out for the help you crave, nor will it serve as your cover of protection.

End the Cover-Up

In the garden when Adam and Eve fell, they discovered their nakedness. Feeling exposed and vulnerable, Eve took fig leaves and fashioned an outfit of sorts to cover her own—and her husband's—"shameful" condition. We do the same thing. We cover our emotional nakedness, ineffectively hiding behind garments of self- protection.

The time has come for a makeover, a new wardrobe. Are you ready to shed those old behaviors? Transformation begins with one word—*Yes!*

Counter-Productive Behaviors

The time has come to get down and dirty and admit that you act in ways that are counter-productive to your emotional health and well-being. Like a butterfly that no longer needs its confining cocoon, you no longer need survival behaviors. Instead of returning to your victim mindset and your obsolete arsenal of coping skills to serve as your emotional and psychological crutches, allow yourself to be stretched higher, pulled deeper, and expanded beyond your current capacity.

> *There is freedom waiting for you,*
> *On the breezes of the sky,*
> *And you ask 'What if I fall?'*
> *Oh but my darling,*
> *What if you fly?* —ERIN HANSON

So how, precisely, do survivors act out in order to deal with the abuse? The following list of addictions and coping behaviors suggests some choices they frequently make:

1. Alcoholism
2. Overeating
3. Shopping, spending money
4. Sex
5. Pornography
6. Lying
7. Manipulation
8. Temper tantrums
9. Control and domination
10. Insecurity, jealousy, comparing
11. Mood swings
12. Immaturity

You may have learned to protect yourself from harm by adopting these or other negative behaviors. They may have become habits confining you to a life of captivity. But there is hope for healing. With intentional work and counseling, you can be set free from hurtful behavioral patterns.

Masks and Shields

You've held on to your victim identity for so long that you may have begun to wonder who you'll be after you begin healing. But don't let that kind of uncertainty stop you. You're shedding the false image to which you've clung for so long so that you may emerge the beautiful person God created and intended you to be. Think of it this way: a beautiful sculpture starts out as a misshapen piece of stone. As the Master chisels away the excess protrusions of rock, the form and beauty of the masterpiece within begin to appear. It was there all the time, but its wonder was obscured.

The goal of healing is to chip off those superfluous edges.

In addition to negative behaviors and acting out, survivors also learn to live behind masks and to hold up defensive shields. Some of the most common include:

The Tough Girl

Determined never to be hurt again, this survivor takes on a hard exterior, rooted in fear. She's terrified of being vulnerable. After all, when she trusted and was open, she was violated. Vowing never to be wounded again, she protects herself with a prickly exterior that broadcasts her message: "Don't come close. I'll hurt you!" The real, unspoken message in that challenge: "Don't hurt me."

The Party Girl

The party girl uses sexuality to anesthetize her pain. She dissociates her body from her pain, and her denial system broadcasts "I haven't been hurt by my past." Unprocessed emotions continue to propel her to act out. She reasons, "Bad attention is better than no attention." This party girl—perhaps engaging in pornography, chat-rooms, group sex, one-night stands, or prostitution—usually stops acting out once therapy starts. In other words, acting out has never been her true desire. Her sexual "freedom" is really no freedom at all but a manifestation of damaged self-esteem, identity confusion, and anger. Subconsciously, she may be using others in much the same way she was used. In her mind her behavior is payback for the wrong done to her.

The Martyr

The martyr is the eternal victim. She controls her environment by acting weak, incapable, sickly, and fragile. She may be the hypochondriac, the one who's plagued with endless symptoms. She wants and needs attention but refuses to admit it. Instead she may stage—not always purposely or knowingly—episodes of weakness and breakdown in order to gain the attention of family and friends. She thrives on crisis and creates an atmosphere of chaos, while casting herself continuously in the role of victim. If this sounds like you, you may be manifesting the symptoms of martyrdom.

The Peacekeeper

Peacekeepers keep peace at all costs, even at the expense of their own needs. They wear a shield of self-sacrifice, not wanting anyone to suspect their real needs—emotionally, sexually, or physically. Their role is that of a fixer: a compliant, selfless, non-burdensome woman. I've worn this mask. I struggled with acknowledging needs. My need of someone else, after all, implies that I'm obligated to allow them to help me, and I feel unworthy of that help. I've struggled for a long time with letting myself become vulnerable.

If this peacemaker is you, you'll recognize the perception that if you can save the day or be the hero you'll be happy. Being the family savior (you might substitute the workplace or some other group) takes the focus off your perceived deficits and recasts you as a selfless and perpetually giving person. You fill your void of self-worth by pleasing other people, keeping quiet about your own needs, and sacrificing for the sake of everyone else.

The Overachiever

Broken self-esteem can manifest itself in our attempt to overachieve. Perhaps your gnawing sense of unworthiness and inadequacy motivates you to prove your worth by achievements. Poor self-esteem drives you to perform intensely in an effort to feel accepted and valued. Even when you have found approval in the eyes of others, do you push yourself to accomplish just a little bit more? Do you compare yourself to others in the always futile and elusive hope that you'll rise above the rest with your successes?

In the end, overachievers develop a neatly constructed façade in the hope that it will hide their deep insecurities, but they continue to doubt their own worth, no matter how well they perform.

The Underachiever

The fear of inadequacy can leave abuse survivors paralyzed by depression and/or haunted by thoughts of failure. They may reject challenges for personal growth and choose the path of least resistance. Broken self-esteem can cause survivors to settle for jobs far beneath their level of ability or for relationships that are unhealthy and plagued with problems.

A low opinion of yourself can perpetuate a life characterized by poor choices and devastating mistakes. The deeply rooted message "You're unworthy of anything good" often plays in the recesses of our minds, and we frequently live in accordance with this subconscious belief.

In his book *The Search for Significance* Robert S. McGee identities four specific false beliefs to which many of us hold in the hope of gaining self-esteem:

+ *I must meet certain standards in order to feel good about myself.*
+ *Others must approve of me and accept me in order for me to feel good about myself.*
+ *Those who fail are unworthy of love and must be punished.*
+ *I am what I am. I can't change. I'm helpless and hopeless.*[30]

The Gender Mask

"Am I gay?"

The stranger's eyes pierced mine as a tear rolled down her cheek. I didn't know her, but her question was familiar. She was dressed in baggy jeans and a T-shirt, wearing a baseball cap backward. A cigarette clung to her lower lip. At first glance I'd thought she was a boy.

"Why do *you think* you're gay?"

"Because I hate men." Her tone was loud and obnoxious.

She informed me that her name was Shane. Her abuse had been vulgar and degrading. It had included penetration with a coat hanger, the handle of a mirror, and other objects inserted into her vagina by her stepfather. He had also smeared feces on his penis before forcing her to perform oral sex.

The nature of her abuse had been so painful and humiliating that she despised her femininity and hated all men.

When I saw her several months after we had first spoken and after she had sought counseling, her transformation was startling.

"Hey, Pastor Dawn, it's me." Then she whispered, "My real name is Sheyanne."

Sheyenne had chosen to wear a mask. Because of her rage toward men she had convinced herself that she would rather be a boy because she believed her masculine identity conferred on her a sense of power. The mask she wore was more than that of the hardened, lesbian tough girl. She had in essence *become* a man. She had positioned herself in an assumed place of power—like her stepfather—to assure herself that she would never again be at the mercy of an abuser.

Sexual image distortions and confusions are common among survivors. Being or becoming a "sexual being" got us hurt in the first place, so we've sought out a sexual identity we believe we can live with. Some victims try to become asexual—as I've heard it expressed, "just a head walking around." Some take on a lesbian mask, while others choose to manifest as bisexual. Still others indulge in promiscuous sexual behavior of various kinds.

Roadside Check-up

1. Are you ready to lay down your survival behaviors, damaging defense mechanisms, and protective masks? If so, offer this prayer: "Jesus, I come to you and ask for your help. Please reveal to me the survival behaviors, shields, and masks I've been using to cope. I'm ready to

become the authentic person you created me to be. Please empower me to walk in the truth of your Word, as I lay down my weapons of protection. Renew my mind. I place my trust in You, Amen."

2. Journal your thoughts here:

Accept Your Worth and Value

One of the most difficult parts of my healing journey was to come to believe that I was as loved, treasured, and valuable as my mentors repeatedly assured me I was. They showed me verses in God's Word in which He refers to me as His daughter, declares that He lavishes His love on me, and assures me that I am radiant to Him. Still, I discovered that I couldn't hold on to the lies ingrained in my psyche and accept the truth at the same time. These two elements were at odds with each other. Although I *felt* as though I were often stupid and unworthy, I began to recognize that those feelings of worthlessness stemmed from Satan's lies and were not founded in Truth.

I had to make a decision, based not on feelings—which are untrustworthy and fickle—but on the authority of the Bible. I wrote these words on my mirror and read them aloud every day: "The truest thing about me? I am who HE SAYS I am." I renewed and washed my mind with the water of God's Word. That meant that I had to give up my false beliefs and coping patterns of thought and admit, "I'm loved. I'm valuable. In fact, "I'm flat out awesome!" (See Psalm 34:5; Romans 12:2; Ephesians 5:26; 1 John 3:1.)

You, too, will have to give up your self-protective beliefs.

No More Denial

Now that you're refusing to regurgitate the party line—"It never happened," or "It wasn't really abuse"—now that you're refusing to deny the pain of your abuse and the reality of the deep wound it left in you—it's time to reclaim what's true and what's yours by creation and redemption. You're worth the time God wants to invest in healing and making you new. He created you with purpose and great value, and He's redeeming everything you've gone through to give you a new, healthy, and whole life.

No More Minimization

Minimization is a thinking distortion. So get over saying things like
Abuse didn't really affect me that much.
I'm over it anyway.
It wasn't that big of a deal.
I forgave, so I'm okay now.
Minimizing your pain and trauma is a way of saying "I'm not worth the hassle. Don't make a big deal over a loser like me. I probably deserved it anyway."

No more of this. You *are* a big deal! You're God's daughter, and He fights for you. No one should ever lay a hand on you without your consent— you're worthy of respect, dignity, and considerate treatment.

No More Comparison

Another thinking distortion we tell ourselves in order to cope is *Compared to others, my abuse wasn't much. I shouldn't complain. It could've been worse.* We tend to make comparisons such as:
Compared to her I got off easy.
I didn't get it as bad as . . .
Others have endured so much worse.
Thinking like this dismisses your personhood. Not to mention that it's a lie. You're saying, in effect, *I don't deserve to complain because others have it worse than I do. So buck up and get over it.*

The reality is that your abuse was deeply personal and painful. It happened to you and should never be compared to anyone else's experience. Their pain is irrelevant to your situation. What happened to you has changed your life forever. You alone get to define how deeply it wounded you. For true healing to come you need to process your memories and talk about them. Affirm yourself by acknowledging your pain.

No More Refusal

The time has come for you to feel *for you*. How can you empathize and care for others if you won't care for yourself? What good does it do to try to put yourself in someone else's shoes if you refuse to walk in your own? Grieve for YOU. Care for YOU. I'm not suggesting a narcissistic existence in which life is "all about you." That's an error in balance in the opposite direction. But do take the time to grieve for how you were hurt and what was stolen from you. Find your voice. Cry. Feel. Heal. You're that important.

— *Part 4* —

DANCING IN TRIUMPH

Finding the Free after Healing

UNLEASHING FORGIVENESS

Forgiving Yourself, Others, and God

Forgiveness is the fragrance the violet sheds on the heel that has crushed it. —ANCIENT ORIGIN WITH NUMEROUS RESTATEMENTS

You've been crushed.

Abuse has ground your flowering soul like pestle grinds a mortar. The fragrance rises and fills the air. It emanates from you and swirls about you. Your essence. Your scent.

But your essence can emanate beauty or darkness—the sweetness of perfume or the stench of decay. What makes the difference?

You. Your decisions, whether bitter or sweet, determine the aroma you bring to the world around you. The secret to infusing the world with fragrance is encapsulated in one powerful word: *forgiveness*.

What Is Forgiveness?

Forgiveness is the deliberate and conscious decision to release feelings of resentment, hatred, and vengeance toward the person or persons who have harmed and wounded you, regardless of whether or not they're deserving of the act of forgiveness have asked for your forgiveness.

"But why should I forgive someone who did such awful things to me [or to someone I love]?" you may ask. "You have no idea what I've been through!"

Yes, I hear you. And no, I don't know what you've been through. But I do know that lack of forgiveness and bitterness keep people's eyes focused backward into the past. Lack of forgiveness literally makes people sick and is classified in medical books as a disease. According to Dr. Steve

Standiford, chief of surgery at the Cancer Treatment Centers of America, "Refusing to forgive makes people sick and keeps them that way."[31]

Forgiveness empowers you to acknowledge and grieve your pain and losses; heal; move forward, unburdened by pain; and refuse to be defined by your abuse. In short, forgiveness sets us free.

In fact, if we look back to the use of the word in Greek, we find that it literally means "to unbind" or "to let go."

When we forgive, we let go of our right to hold a grudge.

We let go of our demand for vindication or repayment.

We release our daydreams of justifiable paybacks.

Once we're released from those chains we're freed, and our desire for revenge or wishing for bad things to happen to the people who've hurt us begins to fade away.

> To forgive is to set a prisoner free and discover that the prisoner was you.
> —LOUIS B. SMEDES

Think about it: you forgive *for you*. Refusing to forgive is like refusing to take a shower and walking around in filth after someone has spent years smearing vile, rotting trash all over you. Yet, despite the power of forgiveness to heal and free us, some survivors still protest, asking through clenched teeth, "Why on earth should I forgive? *I'll never* forgive them for what they did!"

Maybe that's still your response. If so, I understand your hesitation because for many years I misunderstood the nature of forgiveness. Here's what I've learned since then:

What Forgiveness Is Not

Forgiveness Isn't Forgetting

True forgiveness isn't a memory lapse. It doesn't mean that you'll magically forget all your hurt and trauma. If at long last you've recovered your buried memories, in fact, you've actually received another portion of your healing. Deep hurts can't be erased or wiped out by our refusal to acknowledge that they ever happened. The power of forgiveness is in the remembering. In the face of hard facts, forgiveness says, "I choose to let go, to relinquish my right to hurt you back for hurting me." Forgiveness then, is a memory *release*. Many survivors find that once they've processed and forgiven the offense they're released from the haunting reoccurrence of memories and the sting of pain associated with recollection of their abuse.

Forgiveness Isn't Reconciliation

Forgiveness definitely doesn't mean that you have to be reconciled to your abuser. In some cases resuming a relationship with the one who has hurt you would invite more abuse. Reconciliation isn't required for authentic forgiveness to take place. An injured party can forgive an offender without the offender ever knowing—whether, in fact, the perpetrator is deceased or alive.

In cases, however, when reconciliation is desirable, forgiveness paves the way for making it possible. Bear in mind, however, that forgiveness doesn't equate to instant trust in anyone who has hurt you.

Forgiveness Isn't Excusing Bad Behavior

What happened to you is inexcusable; the crime against you will never be *okay*. Releasing someone from his or her sin against you isn't an attempt to pass off the assault as inconsequential or insignificant, and the offense is neither thereby condoned nor dismissed. But forgiveness keeps your heart from being destroyed by the abuser and the abusive acts committed against you.

Forgiveness Isn't Absolution

When you finally forgive, the abuser isn't thereby absolved from all consequences. You can, in fact, walk through the process of seeking justice while (or after) forgiving. In many circumstances the offender will face necessary and difficult consequences as a result of their crime, and your forgiveness shouldn't stop an appropriate process whereby justice is served.

Forgiveness Doesn't Have to Be Requested

Some survivors believe that we have to be asked by the offender before we need to (or can) forgive them.

Not true. You can forgive without ever hearing your abuser ask for forgiveness, since forgiveness is about *your* attitude and heart and not about theirs.

It's helpful for us to recall the words and attitude of Jesus on the subject of forgiveness. While His wounds were still fresh and He was bleeding on the cross, our Savior whispered, "Father, forgive them, for they do not know what they are doing" (Luke 23:34). Jesus released forgiveness toward those who had brutalized Him. His words indicate that those He forgave failed to comprehend the enormity of their actions or their eternal impact. It's also clear that they didn't request forgiveness.

As much as you long to hear words like "I violated you. I committed a horrible crime against you. Please forgive me" spoken by the one who devastated you, chances are your ears won't ever hear an expression of repentance from your abuser.

The good news is that your healing and recovery aren't predicated on the repentance of sinful, selfish people. So don't wait for it. Move forward with your life and embrace your beautiful future! As film producer and director Paul Boese puts it, "Forgiveness does not change the past, but it does enlarge the future."

You can also forgive without ever announcing to the perpetrator "I forgive you." If you have the desire and opportunity in an appropriate setting to express your forgiveness, that's fine. But this isn't a prerequisite for true forgiveness.

Forgiveness Isn't Powerlessness

Once you forgive you don't return to the role of a victim. On the contrary—you become empowered. Your abusive perpetrator no longer controls you. Many survivors feel that if they forgive they relinquish their power and means of defense. That, however, is an illusion. The truth is that true power comes when you can look your pain in the face and claim victory over it. And that victory can be yours through forgiveness!

Forgiveness Isn't a Quick Fix

Forgiveness isn't an indication that you're finished healing. Be careful not to falsely assume that real forgiveness means you no longer need to sort out feelings and issues related to your abuse. If you think (as I did), "I've forgiven, so it's all over now," you'll likely thwart your healing process. I wish it were that simple to let go of the past, but I don't believe it is. Forgiving is a necessary part of the healing process, but give yourself permission to revisit the pain, talk through your abuse, and process the residual effects for as long as you need to.

Finally, because forgiveness is such a powerful and freeing force, counselors and mentors are eager for survivors to get to the place where they're ready to let go. But don't rush yourself. You don't want to use forgiveness as a means of avoiding the need to continue processing your trauma. Forgiveness isn't a detour around your pain and brokenness, nor is it a panacea to eradicate the ongoing hurt. Forgive at your own pace.

I made the mistake of forgiving too readily. Well-meaning leaders told me that if I wanted Jesus to forgive me I had to first forgive my dad. I wanted to be free from the past, so before I delved into the depths of my abuse I quickly forgave and slammed the door shut on that aspect of my past.

I thought I'd found the magic bullet to accelerated healing—the short "check-out line" known by only a few. I was finally done with the whole sexual abuse thing. After all, I'd forgiven my dad.

Over the next year or so, however, thoughts of the sexual abuse continued to plague me. Panic attacks and depression randomly popped up as though in a revolting game of peek-a-boo. I felt blindsided and emotionally disabled. But since I'd forgiven, I avoided the notion that I still needed to revisit my childhood trauma. I continued to stuff down the troubling memories and refused to admit that I might not have been "totally healed." I tried—unsuccessfully—to get on with my life.

The problem was that I had misunderstood forgiveness. Easy, cheap forgiveness wasn't an instant remedy or quick fix for my abusive past. I soon discovered that there are no shortcuts on the sexual healing journey. Indeed, there can't be. Forgiveness requires integrity—an honest and rigorous plunge into our deepest pain, worst fears, and vilest anger.

Forgiveness often comes at the end of our grueling grief and healing work, after we have explored the depth of our pain and out-reasoned our seductive rationalizations. That's why I've placed this chapter toward the end of the book, so that you won't feel rushed, coerced, or unprepared to forgive. It's absolutely true that without forgiveness you'll remain a prisoner of your past and a captive of Satan. But shallow, surface forgiveness that fails to acknowledge deep wounds is insufficient for deep spiritual and emotional healing.

◆ ◆ ◆

Break the Ties That Bind

"Forgiveness" comes from the root word *mercy*, which means "to unbind." In ancient times criminals (often murderers) would pay for their crime knowing that *no forgiveness* was possible for them. To demonstrate the permanence of their merciless fate, a dead body was strapped to their backs, binding together the rotting corpse and the criminal. As the body decomposed it would slowly spread decay into the living flesh of the condemned. In the end they both perished, joined bone-to-bone by gangrene.

This is an appalling picture of the binding power of a refusal to forgive. It binds us irrevocably to the injustice committed against us, and to our perpetrator, in a way that ultimately eats away at us until we rot.

However, once we forgive the rottenness of the past falls away and the poison no longer infects us. We're no longer victims chained to our past. We're able to live and flourish in the present. I like to think of it this way: "As a forgiver you become more than a survivor—you're a thriver."

When you hold resentment toward another, you are bound to that person or condition by an emotional link that is stronger than steel. Forgiveness is the only way to dissolve that link and get free. —KATHERINE PONDER

When you cast off the oppressive burden you've carried for so long, the trauma loses its power to control and manipulate your life. Without offering true forgiveness, however, you'll remain stuck in your pain. All the work you've done in your attempt to heal will become futile.

True Forgiveness

As you prepare to forgive, reflect on this summary of what constitutes true forgiveness. Forgiveness is

+ **A Choice.** You can decide to release your ill will and change your thinking about the one who has hurt you, regardless of how you feel.
+ **A Bridge to Healing.** Once you forgive you can return, without fear, to your painful story, perhaps in order to help someone else or to revisit an area of your life that still needs healing.
+ **A Process, Not an Event.** You'll continue to forgive throughout your healing process and, indeed, throughout your life. When new memories surface or new seasons of life trigger you to relive aspects of your trauma, you'll forgive again—a little more deeply each time.
+ **Letting Go.** Forgiveness enables you to release attitudes, emotions, and mindsets that have controlled you as a result of your abuse. You're freed to let negative emotions and thoughts slide away.
+ **Moving Forward.** Forgiveness is a huge step toward embracing your future. You're no longer stuck! Forgiveness removes roadblocks to success.
+ **A Display of Grace.** Forgiveness is miraculous. Beyond our human capability, forgiveness is a display of God's divine love, grace, and forgiveness for us. When you forgive you radiate God's glory.

Forgiving God; Forgiving Me

The two beings we most often forget to forgive are God and ourselves. It isn't actually that we *forget to forgive*. We're typically unaware or in denial of our strong resentment toward God and ourselves. As we arrive at this phase of healing, it's important for us to come clean, to acknowledge our disappointment and resentment against both God and ourselves. Are you prepared to admit "I'm angry!"?

Very angry.

Forgiving God

It may sound sacrilegious to think about the prospect of forgiving God. But forgiving God doesn't imply that He has done something wrong. Of course He hasn't. God is perfect in all His ways. What it does mean is that you've had an expectation—conscious or unconscious—of how a "loving God" should have responded to your abuse. When your expectations weren't met you became angry, resentful, hurt, and confused. You felt as though your trust in *God the Protector* was shattered. You distanced yourself from God, concluding that He is, at least in your personal experience, neither fair nor trustworthy. Does that sound familiar?

Do you grapple with agonizing questions like

Where was God when I was molested?

Why didn't he stop it?

Why would God have allowed my abuse at all?

These questions and others like them point to the reservoir of broken and unresolved emotions of your heart. Since no pat, universal answer or antidote can soothe every wounded heart (though counselors and pastors alike continue resolutely to posit suggestions), your search for resolution to those perplexing questions will serve to connect you with the One who alone can offer peace. Forgiving God is part of answering that burning, universal question, "Where were you when I was being abused?"

As I sought to understand God's attitude toward and response to my abuse, I told myself what I knew to be true about God and His character.

God is faithful.

God is good in all His ways.

God is patient and kind.

God is just.

God is present—up close and personal.

Among other realities I discovered—experientially—that God is love. Let me repeat that, in the unforgettable words of the evangelist John: "God *is* love" (1 John 4:8, emphasis mine). John wasn't stating an attribute God has but a quality He embodies.

I found comfort in believing that God in all of His love was there with me all along, not only protecting my mind from trauma beyond its coping ability but also grieving my grief right along with me (check out Romans 8:26–27 and Hebrews 4:15 on the subject of the Holy Spirit's vicarious grief on our behalf). I learned that God's perfect love endowed each of us with a free will and that, sadly, many use that freedom to hurt others.

I also began to understand that if God were to stop every single person from committing horrific acts of violence against the innocent, we would live in a perfect, flawless world. Why then, would we need a Savior? Jesus would have died in vain. Besides, how could we as automatons love, praise, honor, and obey the Father?

Forgiving Me

Another area of difficulty may be that of forgiving *you*—of giving yourself grace. I was so mixed up about this principle. I easily forgave my father but remained hard as steel with regard to my outlook on myself, offering the hurting me neither mercy nor compassion. Eventually I realized that my lack of self-compassion was actually a lack of forgiveness. I wasn't allowing myself to be freed from my judgments about myself. I couldn't unleash the new Dawn inside me without forgiving the young, innocent Dawn cowering there, wide-eyed and terrified, in the shadows.

An abused child has committed no wrong, and she is never the one to blame. On a logical level you probably agree with me. But, deep inside, are you still captive to your own self-judgments? Perhaps you aren't consciously aware of it, but you may be holding yourself responsible for your sexual assault. You did nothing wrong, but until you forgive yourself *for any perceived wrong or deficit* you will continue to feel culpable.

Why didn't I stop it?

I should have told someone. Maybe then it would have stopped.

That's what I get for being a stupid, gullible kid.

It was my fault for being in the wrong place at the wrong time.

Maybe I asked for it. After all, the attention felt good.

Your endless list of false rationalizations will keep you angry with yourself for a long time. It's time to release yourself from blame and from those unrealistic expectations—to remind yourself emotionally of what you already know rationally: that a child is never to blame for abuse.

Take another important step toward recovery by forgiving yourself today.

Roadside Check-up

Are you Ready?

The most difficult aspect of forgiveness is letting go. Remember that your feelings don't have to line up with your will. The act of forgiveness is just that—a deliberate *act* of your will. If you're ready, forgiveness is yours when you take these steps:

1. Ask God to help you take this step of obedience.
2. Admit that you can't forgive on your own.
3. Trust and rely on God's divine help and strength.
4. Tell God from your heart, out loud, what it is you need to forgive. You may want to have a list prepared to read aloud to God.
5. Acknowledge your negative response and regrettable behaviors after the offense and receive God's cleansing and forgiveness for yourself.
6. Release the offense to God and visualize placing your pain at the foot of the cross of Jesus Christ.
7. Claim your freedom in Christ and walk free.

Some survivors find it helpful to compose a letter to the person who has harmed them. I have heard this called a "poison pen letter." We write the letter not to send but rather as a way to purge our mind and heart of the offense. It's common to recall previously forgotten details during the writing process. You may also come to realize how deep and hidden your pain really is. Some survivors follow through with a ceremony in which they destroy their lists and letters, symbolizing the end of the link between themselves and their offenders. Others visualize placing their list on a raft and watching it drift gently away down a river, while still others burn their letters and scatter the ashes. By using a tangible expression of forgiveness and release similar to one of these, you may be able to find release and separation from your wounds.

Free at Last

Forgiveness is divine and powerful, paving the way for emotional, physical, and spiritual recovery. The wonderful reality is that, no matter what your circumstances, you possess the power to forgive. Once you're freed from the painful chains that have bound you you can move on with your life without the burden of bitterness.

Is *today* your day to be free at last?

— 13 —

FREEING YOUR INNER CHILD
Grieving the Losses of Childhood

My grief and pain are mine. I have earned them. They are part of me.
Only in feeling them do I open myself to the lessons they can teach.
—ANNE WILSON SCHAFF

You've suffered many losses. You've come to the place at which it's time to honor those losses. Think of it this way: in grieving for yourself you pay respect to the human being who endured abuse and paid the price. Grieving for yourself is an act of self-respect, not of self-loathing or disgust. Grieving for yourself helps you leave your anger behind, shed your victim mentality, and move forward to become a hero who understands the value of honor. You've survived, and you deserve to present yourself with a medal.

Grief isn't something to be worn on your sleeve to elicit pity, but you *can* carry it proudly, knowing that you've fought the battle to receive the closure you so desperately needed. Hold your head high, honoring the battle you've fought and the pain you've survived and overcome.

How Do I Grieve?

"But I don't know how to grieve. How do I let go?" I asked my counselor. "I can't cry. I have no tears for myself. I only feel disgusted by the gullible, mute child inside me. She just laid there and took the abuse and never uttered a word."

"That sounds like someone else I know," Amy acknowledged. "Remember how Jesus stood in silence before his accusers? His voice was silent, but He knew that one day his voice would echo from the heavens.

"You survived. You persisted through a demeaning and horrific atrocity. You were degraded and humiliated. Your younger self did what she had to do to make it out alive."

Amy tried to encourage me, but I still bristled at the idea of forgiving that child.

"Tears are for babies and for people who are stupid enough to let themselves get hurt again," I retorted.

"Or perhaps tears are the doorway to finding your voice. Let your child speak, Dawn. She wants to tell you how she felt. The language of a child is tears. Let her speak; let her tell you how she felt. Don't stifle her."

I wasn't trying to stifle her. But I believed that tears rendered me weak and vulnerable, and I couldn't allow that. I needed to stay strong and in control. How could I let my inner child express her feelings and cry without feeling violated all over again?

The reality is that the grieving process requires risk for all of us—the risk of *feeling* violated, afraid, vulnerable, or any other emotion that may feel uncomfortable or unfamiliar (because we've stifled it for so long)—or all too familiar. We might have to numb out to escape those scary, unwanted feelings, and wouldn't that be counterproductive to grieving and healing? But the beauty of grieving is that it *requires us* to feel. The only way *out of pain* is to go *through the pain* via the process of mourning.

As I talked with Amy that day I realized that the way to grieve was to give myself permission to *feel* my emotions and trust that I'd find freedom on the other side of the valley of grief.

With Amy's help I came to recognize that I had to assign my inner a child a new role. She had done such a great job of staying strong and not breaking down that she was afraid by that point to feel anything but anger. She was so numb to other emotions that she didn't know how to *feel* at all. Now it was my turn—as the compassionate adult Dawn—to take over. Little Dawn had taken us as far as she could. It was time for her to rest, put down her weapons, and end her angry vigil. The battle was over. She was free to let go. My role was to comfort, listen to, care for, and help my inner child. I had become the "grown-up" I had always longed for—the one who would hold me and give me loving support.

What about Anger?

Anger may be said to be the front door to the house of mourning. It wouldn't be unusual for you to walk in and out of unresolved anger on your journey to recovery. Once you're able to lock the door behind you and sit down to rest, you can finally grieve. Anger and bitterness are often transformed to tears of freedom and release as you empathize with the wounded child within you.

When I at long last released my anger, my grieving finally began. My next step was to honestly face my pain and losses. I had to acknowledge each piece of my soul that had been stripped from me.

After my listing of losses was complete, I recognized my inner child's losses and told her how truly sad I was on her behalf. I acknowledged her pain, assuring her that she deserved to feel sad and that it was okay for her to cry. A gush of tears rose and broke through from some deep, unknown recesses in my soul—places "little Dawn" knew only too well. I grieved with her and complimented her on how strong she had been. I asked her for forgiveness—for my being too harsh on her and blaming her. I assured her that I loved her and that I wanted us to be integrated and whole.

It was at the point that I made a discovery: when you can finally grieve, old wounds begin to heal.

That doesn't mean that anger won't ebb and flow during the grief process; it most definitely will. When I recognized the enormity of what I'd lost, I was justifiably furious all over again. But the bitter grip of caustic anger began to loose its hold as I finally let go and grieved.

Is it time for you to grieve? Can you begin to number the losses you've experienced? I placed the following on my own list:

Loss of Childhood

We were children, unsuspecting and trusting. We wanted to laugh at the clouds and dance in the rain like other kids. But something awful happened that interrupted our carefree lives. We stood covered in shame and peered at others through hollow eyes, wondering whether anyone knew, whether anyone else could tell.

Our childhoods had been stolen.

I recall one support group session at which we were discussing childhood memories. Jen spoke with sarcasm: "Childhood? What childhood? All I can remember is the wooden floor in my bedroom. I spent most of my time under the bed hiding from my stepfather. If that's what you mean by childhood—staring at the grain in the wooden slats—then I had a long one."

Grieving the death of childhood happens in four stages:

Denial: "I'm okay. It wasn't really all that bad. Besides, it's over now, and I'm just fine. I didn't really miss out on anything. My parents did their best. I'm sure they loved me in their way."

Anger: "I hate them for what they did to me. I want to pay them back for hurting me. And why me, anyway? It was all so unfair! They used their power to crush me. Authority does that. I hate them. I didn't deserve to lose my childhood. Now I'll be screwed up forever."

Depression: "I never was given real love. Other kids have parents who love them. But not me—no one has ever loved me. My life is hopeless and meaningless—so what's the point? I never got to dream as a kid. I was too busy surviving. It's not about self-pity; it's just as fact. My life is useless. I have no purpose. No dreams. I'm lost. Most days I just want to die."

Acceptance: "I have to accept the loss. It wasn't my fault—my childhood wasn't under my control. I didn't have all the wonderful experiences other kids have, but I can choose to make my adult life happy. I can take the pain of what happened and turn it into an opportunity to grow. I can find comfort and healing as I process my pain, and I can use what I've learned to help someone else.

Roadside Check-up

1. Take a moment and think about where you are in the four stages of grief. Write out your thoughts if you find it helpful.

2. What could you do to move yourself closer to acceptance?

3. Read the Serenity Prayer, below. If you're ready, make it *your* prayer, right now:

God, grant me the serenity to accept the things I cannot change, the courage to change the things I can, and the wisdom to know the difference. Amen.
—REINHOLD NIEBUHR

Loss of Love and Nurture

To children, nurture plus protection equals love. Every child deserves not only to *be* loved but also to *feel* love. Acceptance and nurture provide the foundation on which children build their sense of safety and security. And every child deserves to be safeguarded from the atrocities of the world.

We looked to our parents and to other trusted adults to protect us, shelter us, and meet our emotional needs. But instead of being cherished we felt abandoned, neglected, and unloved.

We can't always blame parents for their children's abuse. Many parents are unaware of the harm done to their children. But something was stolen from us nevertheless—something that can never be replaced. Abused children live in isolation—with a secret that separates them from the love and nurture of other members of their family and community.

In circumstances like mine—in which a parent has abused his or her own child—the loss of nurture is unfathomable. I felt alone. If anyone were going to take care of me, it was going to have to be me. No one else took an interest in my needs, nor could they: they had no idea what my particular needs were. I wasn't about to burden my mother by being needy, so I learned to become self-sufficient and strong.

Many survivors feel this way. Depriving a child of nurture conditions her to protect and nurture herself. She often builds an impenetrable fortress— walls intended to protect but that instead close her off from any opportunity to accept love and care.

Loss of Memory

I love watching my children—now all adults and married—come together for family events. They laugh hysterically as they reflect back on their childhood memories. It thrills my heart to watch and listen to them and to know that, because of God's grace, they can look back on fulfilling childhoods. They have a priceless gift: happy memories.

Our memories, both positive and negative, remind us of who we are and from where we've come. Our history is part of our identity.

But for survivors critical pieces of childhood experience are missing, and subconsciously selected memories are completely forgotten. The pain and trauma of abuse were too much for our tender psyche, and we blocked them out. The downside to repressing our memories, known as psychological amnesia, is that it can wipe out pleasant memories as well.

The loss of many of my memories was another significant casualty for me as a result of my abusive past. Because important pieces of my childhood were missing from my recall, I floundered in an attempt to "find myself." Maybe you, too, sense a loss of identity and unique purpose. You've been ripped off in that way, too.

Loss of Control

Prior to my healing I often wondered why in situations in which I was denied choices I reacted with anger. It has always been important for me to have a voice in any decision-making process. I've discovered that the need for control is common among those who've been sexually exploited.

As children we were overpowered; others stripped us of our right and ability to choose. We silently surrendered to the humiliation of sexual assault while we inwardly screamed. We learned to recognize that our voice was meaningless. As an adult I came to realize that I battled feelings of insignificance. I wondered whether my desires or wishes mattered to anyone.

Is this true for you?

Attempting to validate themselves, many female survivors overexert their wills, determined never to be silenced again. I understand why. I'd rather err on the side of belligerence than run the risk of being violated again.

On the other end of the spectrum, however, women sometimes choose to be overly passive and dependent. Even though they are intelligent, inside they still feel small, inadequate, and insignificant.

I talked to one bright, witty woman who was in her recovery process. I'll call her Sue. I was surprised when she shared, "I'm paralyzed when I need to make decisions because I don't trust myself. If anything, I have an uncanny ability to choose the wrong thing." Because she was forced to forfeit control over her body, her most sacred possession, she questioned her ability to discern right from wrong. "I'm always confused. I'd like to trust my instincts, but I'm afraid my instincts are bad."

Her helpless affect communicated that "I'm incapable of taking care of myself. I need you in order to survive." Although it may seem ironic, passive dependence was her way of gaining control. It said, "I'm released from the responsibility of life and choose to rely on you to make decisions for me." In her mind, her response forced others to take responsibility for her choices and absolved her of liability.

Loss of Purpose and Self-Esteem

I floundered as a young adult. I wondered why I couldn't find my purpose and struggled with self-worth.

Abuse had robbed me of healthy, positive self-esteem. Bear in mind that children practice "magical" thinking and unconsciously assess their value based on the love and nurture they receive.

If someone more powerful than ourselves—an authority figure—assaulted us, we assumed that the abuse was our fault. After all, we're required to respect adults; they're always right and know "what's best for us." The obvious conclusion for a naive and trusting child is "I must be bad."

When as children we evaluated ourselves and decided that WE, not our abusers, were bad and naughty, we began to suffer the lifelong consequences of too often irreparably damaged self-esteem. Degrading sexual assault steals yet a second piece of the victim's soul: our ability to feel loved, accepted, and valued. But in spite of these losses in my own life I'm thankful for a loving God who reveals to us the true beauty and value of who we are. In Christ we are radiant! (Psalm 34:5).

Loss of Trust

Unfortunately, loss of trust is virtually universal among abuse victims and one of the saddest losses of our ordeal.

You and I were betrayed in the most personal and intimate way. We felt utterly abandoned, and we carried our secret alone.

Living without the ability to trust anyone else is painful. It's also impractical, since our very existence depends on trusting others. To survive, many survivors fantasize about the goodness of another person and recast them as a hero; they can be blind to flaws in people to whom they have assigned the hero role. They can, on the other hand, also be too quick to mistrust. As a result survivors blur reality, confuse loyalties, and mistrust others.

Survivors also struggle with the inability to trust themselves. I was unsure of myself and of my ability to make good choices. Like Sue, above, we survivors can lose faith in ourselves because our self-confidence has been eroded. We frequently wonder whether our perceptions and judgments are sound. *Are my feelings accurate,* we wonder, *or is my thinking twisted?*

This inability to trust others and ourselves follows us into our adult lives, threatening our relationships. Because trust is the foundation for all intimacy, impaired trust obstructs the closeness we desire with one another and were designed to achieve.

My ability to trust was eroded during childhood and continued to crumble into my adult life, especially in my marriage. My words weren't meant to sound threatening, but my husband felt uncomfortable when I informed him of my need for him to help me trust him. He felt frustrated that I couldn't demonstrate blind confidence in him when his behaviors felt destructive and damaging to me. When he hid things from me, he'd explain by saying "I'm trying to protect you," but I felt deceived, not protected. Trust—or, more accurately, the lack of trust—was a toxic wedge between us.

For me trust equaled respect. So when I couldn't trust I acted disrespectfully.

Loss of Sexual Enjoyment

Sexual intimacy was distorted for me as a result of sexual abuse. How could I view sex in the way God intended—as pure and beautiful—when I'd been introduced to it in a perverse, twisted manner? A survivor's perspective on the true purpose and role of sex becomes distorted.

I was riddled with triggers—excruciating memories, flashbacks, fears, and anger during sexual encounters. I longed to enjoy intimate moments with my husband, but I felt as though my abuser were with us in bed, too. Before I could receive loving and caring touches I had to fight off troubling flashbacks.

My struggle with painful memories in those moments didn't lead to great romance. I couldn't quiet the noise of the past long enough to enter the beauty of the present.

My healing has been in process for more than twenty years now, and today I'm very capable of giving and receiving sexual intimacy and touch. I've learned the God-intended beauty of sex. Be assured that there is hope for those who struggle with sexual intimacy.

The loss of sexual freedom in romance was one more way in which abuse had robbed me. Sexual intimacy was created to be one of the most precious gifts a husband and wife can share. But for husbands and wives with abuse in one or both of their pasts, making love often feels anything but loving.

Jerry described to me his heartbreak over lack of sexual intimacy with his wife, Sandy. She was having problems expressing herself sexually, stating that she "felt dirty." When Jerry made sexual advancements toward her she shrugged him off, rolled over, and pretended to be asleep.

"I hate her father," Jerry spat out as he slammed his fist into his other hand. "His selfish acts of lust didn't just steal from my wife sexually. He stole from me. He's ruined both our lives."

Sandy was hurting, too. She longed to share intimacy with her husband but felt compelled to continuously avoid sex with Jerry. On nights when she could no longer refuse him she fought to stay present during sex. "I feel like I'm having an out-of-body experience, as if it's happening to someone else. I'm at the top of the room looking down on it all." Sandy was disassociating—severing her emotions from her actions—while having sex. Dissociation is one of many symptoms of sexual dysfunction. While you're in the process of recovery you will likely experience at least some of the following:

+ Difficulty being aroused and feeling enjoyable sensations.
+ Negative feelings, such as guilt, shame, fear, anger, outrage, or disgust, when being touched.
+ Disturbing sexual thoughts and images.
+ Hatred toward sex or feeling as though engaging in sex is an obligation.
+ Inappropriate sexual behaviors or sexual compulsivity.
+ Inability to achieve orgasm.
+ Detachment or emotional distance while having sex.
+ Fear or avoidance of sex.

These were my losses, and I cried for myself over each and every one.

There is a sacredness in tears. They are not the mark of weakness, but of power. They speak more eloquently than ten thousand tongues. They are the messengers of overwhelming grief, of deep contrition, and of unspeakable love.
—WASHINGTON IRVING

Roadside Check-up

1. Find a quiet place and allow yourself to reflect on your losses. Write them down if you desire.

2. Explore the experiences that have been stolen from you. Write them down.

3. What would you tell someone else who has lost these things?

4. Tell yourself the same things and give yourself permission to grieve for yourself.

DANCING INTO THE FREE
Overcoming Your Giants by Faith

I have also learned that because of pain, I can feel the beauty, tenderness, and freedom of healing. Pain feels like a fast stab wound to the heart. But then healing feels like the wind against your face when you are spreading your wings and flying through the air! We may not have wings growing out of our backs, but healing is the closest thing that will give us that wind against our faces. —C. JOYBELL C.

I'm not certain I've healed completely. I'm not even sure I will recognize full healing if and when it comes. But I do know one thing: waves of immense joy splash over me, seemingly out of nowhere, more frequently than I've ever before experienced. It happens when I'm in the grocery store or doing a load of laundry. It happens when I'm preaching or sitting, idle, in a traffic jam. No matter what I'm doing, I frequently feel God's smile on my life and the wind of the Holy Spirit sweeping through me and filling me. The joy of the Lord truly has become my strength.

For me, this is healing. I've become strong at the broken places. My triggers are, for the most part, gone. I have peace.

I've walked the healing journey with all of its winding roads and hazards, and I've found freedom.

It's mine.

I may not always appear to others to be healed. I'm not perfect. I may still have a limp in my step or a scar on my soul, but I've walked the walk, and now I can run. And fly. And even soar.

I've danced out of the darkness into the free, into the light. I do more than exist. I live life to the full.

This is my prayer for you as well. This is your time, your moment to shed the past. Take off the combat boots. You've slogged too long through the trenches. Instead, lace up your slippers and dance in to wholeness. Your soul longs to move with the rhythm of grace.

I
I walk down the street.
There is a deep hole in the sidewalk.
I fall in
I am lost. . . . I am helpless
It isn't my fault.
It takes forever to find a way out.

II
I walk down the same street.
There is a deep hole in the sidewalk.
I pretend I don't see it.
I fall in again
I can't believe I am in the same place, but it isn't my fault.
It still takes a long time to get out.

III
I walk down the same street
There is a deep hole in the sidewalk.
I see it there.
I still fall in. . . . it's a habit, my eyes are open.
I know where I am.
It is my fault.
I get out immediately.

IV
I walk down the same street.
There is a deep hole in the sidewalk.
I walk around it.

V
I walk down another street.
—PORTIA NELSON

The time has come for you to walk down that other street. Life is offering you a new path—a path that offers you the opportunity to run and dance, to flourish and thrive.

But you protest, "I've never walked this way before. Where do I start? What if I don't know *how* to dance into the free?"

That's okay—just take baby steps. You can even crawl into the new, fresh, open space if you need to. Just start by moving ahead one inch, one small decision at a time!

To help you along, I want to provide a few guiding principles from my playbook for tackling life and healing. I call these guidelines my "Super Seven"—seven life-changing promises I've made to myself—and I invite you to use them and create some of your own as well.

1. I Will Be Brave.

It's fine, and even normal, to periodically experience feelings of fear, failure, and discouragement. Don't expect to be completely rid of those troublesome emotions. They'll still rise up from time to time and talk trash to you. You know—telling you your life was all about defeat and failure, reminding you of your past, shaming you out of your future. So when fear and failure talk remind them (and yourself) who and where you are today: "Today I'm free. I choose a new path and a new attitude. I allow myself to remember my past, to grieve, and to feel righteous anger, but I'm not a slave to my feelings. I'm not paralyzed by my emotions."

> *It takes courage . . . to endure the sharp pains of self discovery rather than choose to take the dull pain of unconsciousness that would last the rest of our lives.*
> —MARIANNE WILLIAMSON, *Return to Love*

Turn Down a New Road

Speak out the following truths with conviction, repeating as often as necessary:

"I am free."

"I am courageous."

"I am bold and fearless."
"Today, I will be brave."

2. I Will Be Gentle.

Dawn, be gentle with yourself, I remind myself frequently.

Gentleness is the quality of being kind, compassionate, and careful, in this case in dealing with yourself. This tenderness is a gift you give to *you*. As you dance into the free you'll find that you have a new partner called *grace*. You may be afraid to accept this life-giving partner at first, but let her do the leading. You'll probably step on her toes, and maybe even trip and fall back into your self-condemning, self-shaming ways, but that's okay. You're en route, on your way to a healthier and happier future. Eventually you'll become convinced that you deserve mercy and gentleness, and you'll learn to dance with grace into the free and to be gentle with both yourself and others.

Turn Down a New Road

Saying—and then following through by doing—the following will help you develop gentleness:

"I will speak to myself with love."
"I will feel what I am feeling in honor of myself."
"I will take one day at a time and celebrate baby steps."
"Today, I will be gentle."

3. I Will Be Patiently Tenacious.

As you move into freedom you'll find another pair of unlikely dance partners: patience and tenacity. Change won't come easily; renewing your mind to live from a new script takes time.

And process. So don't forget to grab these two virtues by the hand as you go.

Patience allows the process of healing to unfold in a way that is truly transformative. Don't force yourself to be better faster, or stronger more quickly. Be patient. Give yourself the time to learn a new way of thinking, feeling, and living. Be tenacious—as I often put it, "like a bull-dog with a dishrag." Don't quit by letting go of your dreams or settling for the status quo. Be fierce about your healing; claim it and confront discomfort when you face it.

If you do quit and give up, that's okay, too—for a minute. Then dust yourself off and start again, remembering the guideline above: "I will be gentle."

The nose of the bulldog is slanted backwards so he can continue to breathe without letting go. —WINSTON CHURCHILL

Turn Down a New Road

When you feel tempted to quit, promise yourself to be patient with the healing process. Then repeat and follow through with the following:
"I will keep trying without condemnation."
"I will be tenacious and receive my freedom."
"I can do all things through Christ who gives me strength."
"Today, I will be tenaciously patient."

4. I Will Own My Story

Researcher and storyteller Brene Brown eloquently observes, "Owning our story and loving ourselves through that process is the bravest thing we'll ever do . . . but I know that it takes more than courage to own your story. We own our stories so we don't spend our lives being defined by them or denying them. And while the journey is long and difficult at times, it is the path to living a more wholehearted life."[32]

I want to live wholeheartedly, so I share my story. You want to live with your whole heart too, or you wouldn't have started this journey.

Ironically, bringing into the open what may be the most humiliating piece of our story frees us from shame and secrecy. Once the light penetrates those dark recesses they no longer seem mysterious and threatening.

Refuse to be ashamed of your story. It happened to you. It's your history, but bear in mind that your story is ultimately an integral part of

HIStory. Give your past to God, allowing Him to redeem it and make it beautiful.

I share my story and own my past. I'm not defined by my experiences; rather, God and I define their meaning in my life. I've been *shaped* by my painful childhood experiences, yes—but not *shamed* by them. I've taken the ashes of disgrace and exchanged them for God's beauty and grace, and I'll see to it from now on that only He gets the glory.

Owning our story without shame affords us the opportunity to connect with others who may be suffering in silent pain. Owning our story inspires others to emerge with us into the light and to own their stories, too.

> *In weakness and shamefulness is also the potential for transcendence, heroism or redemption.* —SCOTT STOSSEL

Turn Down a New Road

Have you owned your story—exchanged the ashes for God's beauty?
Here's what I say:
"I own my story without shame."
"I am not defined by my past."
"I share my story with courage so that God's beauty may be seen."
"Today, I will own my story."

5. I Will Use My Voice.

You're *worthy* of a voice, so allow your unique expressive style to flow freely. Don't let fear silence you. Your ideas, feelings, thoughts, beliefs, and dreams matter. Because your voice keeps you connected to the world around you, using it keeps you present and engaged. Everything about your life and relationships will grow and flourish as you tap in to the power of your personal voice.

Since you live in freedom, you've learned that your voice—representing the sum of your ideas, thoughts, and desires—is different from anyone else's. YOU get to choose how and when to share. You get to decide whether you prefer to sit in quiet solitude or to speak, sing, laugh, or cry out your feelings. Expressing yourself may feel awkward at first, but speak up and be confident. You have something of value to add to the world around you.

When you give yourself permission to communicate what matters to you in every situation you will have peace despite rejection or disapproval. Putting a voice to your soul helps you to let go of the negative energy of fear and regret.
—SHANNON L. ALDER

Turn Down a New Road

Your voice—representing your feelings, thoughts, and beliefs—is yours. It's good for you to be unique, unlike anyone else. So determine to speak out and follow through with action:
"I will use my voice."
"My voice is important."
"My voice is unique, and that's a good thing."
"Today, I will use my voice."

6. I Will Embrace Vulnerability.

When I first considered the idea of allowing myself to be vulnerable, I bristled. Just thinking about opening myself up gave me the chills. *I should stay strong and in control*, protested that wary inner self. The thought of laying down my shield and sword, of knowing that someone could—at any time and without forewarning—reach in and grab my heart; shred it to pieces; and thrust my bleeding, wounded heart back into my gaping chest, was scary, to say the least. Yet I somehow sensed that, at the end of that ridiculous, worst case imagined scenario I would still be alive. My heart's steady beating would continue unabated, reliable and strong.

I'd seen through the myth of vulnerability.

We suspect that vulnerability is weakness and expect it to be our undoing, often viewing it as an inroad for more hurt and pain. Yet my own perceived invincibility was rendering me weak.

I no longer equate vulnerability with weakness or danger. On the contrary, I know that it makes us incredibly strong. Allowing ourselves to be exposed and open is part of being courageous. You can't truly experience life without being willing to open yourself up to others. Being vulnerable means willing yourself to be known, to be authentic. Vulnerability without dishonor is a beautiful revelation of who you are, and it's the only environment in which true love can thrive.

No matter how hard we try to create a mystique of invincibility, the truth is that, if we're going to engage in life and run into the free, we'll still find ourselves susceptible to injury. That's life. But healthy vulnerability unleashes in us the amazing capacity to be connected to and enthralled by life in the most fulfilling way imaginable.

Turn Down a New Road

Become a friend to your own vulnerability. You'll discover strength you never knew you had. I tell myself:

"I can do this. I am not afraid to be known."

"God is with me. He makes me confident."

"In vulnerability I am beautifully strong."

"Today, I will be vulnerable."

To love at all is to be vulnerable. Love anything, and your heart will certainly be wrung and possibly broken. If you want to make sure of keeping it intact, you must give your heart to no one, not even to an animal. Wrap it carefully round with hobbies and little luxuries; avoid all entanglements; lock it up safe in the casket or coffin of your selfishness. But in that casket—safe, dark, motionless, airless— it will change. It will not be broken; it will become unbreakable, impenetrable, irredeemable. —C. S. LEWIS

7. I Will Risk Failure.

Failure doesn't decimate me the way it used to.

I suppose this is because my self-esteem used to hinge on what I perceived to be my perfect performance. I was afraid to swing into new territory or try something I'd never done before because I couldn't afford to fail. Failure most certainly would have meant a loss of face, value, worth, and—worst of all—significance. *Then* who would want me? No, I needed to perform impeccably in every area to be worthy of love. No room for trial and error, stumbling, limited or provisional success—or failure!

Wow. What a vicious cycle we set up for ourselves!

But today I risk failure. I've accepted that failure is a part of life—for all of us. And the sooner we accept this truth the better and the more effective we'll become. When the paralyzing fear of imperfection is shattered, we enter into life with new freedom and zest. We become participants—players instead of spectators or armchair critics. As survivors, we've spent enough time on the sidelines watching everyone else "have it all." It's our turn to get off the bench and onto the field—our turn to get out there and give it our best shot.

When we were kids all gussied up in our "Sunday" best, we were told that we had to sit still and that there was to be no "rough-housing." We would be in big trouble if we messed up our pristine outfits. I vividly recall one Sunday, however, when our Sunday school class went outside to play and I ended up with a grass stain on my dress. When my mom saw it she shrugged it off, dismissively exclaiming, "Oh well, you might as well go play. I'll have to wash it anyway."

What freedom. What joy. Unshackled from the fear of failing to "stay perfect," I was unleashed into the wide-open spaces to frolic without a care in the world.

Right now God is saying that it's okay for you to go outside and play. He's setting you free from having to sit still and worry about your immaculate outside image.

So go play!

Engage in life.

If you fall down, God will be there to pick you up.

Failure is an event, not an identity. As American screenwriter, Charlie Kaufman, once said, "Failure is a badge of honor. It means you risked failure." Your soul can't come alive unless you take a great risk. Full life can't happen for you apart from risk.

It is no secret that the greatest treasures are found in the most remote, inaccessible and difficult places where we must pursue them with great energy and even greater risk. It's the same with our lives. —CRAIG D. LOUNSBROUGH

Turn Down a New Road

Have you decided that you're ready to live life to the fullest, even if that means risking failure?

Here's what I say:

"My life is an adventure to be lived."

"I will risk failure before I quit and do nothing."

"'Failure' isn't my identity. It's just an event."

"Today, I will risk failure."

Courage doesn't always roar. Sometimes courage is the little voice at the end of the day that says I'll try again tomorrow. —MARY ANNE RADMACHER

◆   ◆   ◆

So now it's up to you. Will you dance into the free? The wide open spaces beckon you to come and experience the life God intended you to live.

You've learned new skills that can help take you to the next level of healing and living free. Don't go backward. I encourage you to continue in this lifelong journey of growing and healing, learning and reaching. You are God's masterpiece, and He wants you to live fully and freely!

The closing chapter of Julie Cantrell's *New York Times* best-selling novel *Into the Free* offers a powerful picture of the journey we've just taken:

Maybe God has always been with me, opening doors, leading me to opportunities, letting me choose my own path, and loving me even when I chose the wrong one. Never giving up on me. Knowing all along that I am on a journey. That I must find my own way to him. Maybe River was right. Maybe God does still believe in me.

In the end . . . I no longer feel afraid; instead, I feel whole and loved and complete, in a way no one like me should ever be able to feel. Not after all I've seen in the world. After all the hurt and hate, fear and fury.[33]

But you can feel loved and complete.
You can soar "into the free."

But me he caught—reached all the way
from sky to sea; he pulled me out
Of that ocean of hate, that enemy chaos,
the void in which I was drowning.
They hit me when I was down,
but God stuck by me.
He stood me up on a wide-open field;
I stood there saved—surprised to be loved!

—PSALM 18:19, MSG

— Appendix 1 —

THE HEALING PROCESS

Healing Stages

How will you know when you're getter stronger? Survivors pass through stages during the healing process. Most therapists recognize and help their clients negotiate these stages. They are common and relatively sequential, but while some survivors experience every stage in the order in which they are listed, many do not. Your experience will be uniquely yours. You probably won't move neatly from one stage to another in exact sequence or predictable time periods. But it's important for you to learn the characteristics of each stage so you can assess at any given point where you are in the healing process.

1. Believing that it happened
2. Deciding to heal
3. Surviving crisis
4. Remembering
5. Choosing to tell
6. Releasing responsibility
7. Finding the inner child
8. Grieving loss
9. Expressing anger
10. Forgiving
11. Resolving the conflict

1. Believing That It Happened
During this stage you come to terms with the fact that you're a survivor of sexual abuse and, as a result, have been profoundly injured. When you're ready to admit that and can say the words out loud, you're ready to travel the road to recovery.

Admitting that you've been harmed and are still being harmed by sexual abuse may seem like an obvious step, but the vast majority of assault survivors minimize their pain or ignore it altogether.

In this first step we acknowledge our abusive past and the damage it has done to our lives. We recognize that we most likely also unknowingly sabotage our present life with destructive behaviors that are rooted in our past.

Sometimes a survivor is willing to look at her pain only because she's forced to. Physical and emotional troubles can suddenly rush into our lives like floodwaters. These symptoms are signals that our surging emotions can't be held in check any longer. Even after we face the realities of our sexual trauma, we may question ourselves and vacillate between "Did it really happen?" and "It wasn't that bad, was it?"

In this stage we choose to shatter denial about our abuse or its impact. We've been dismissing our abuse, shrugging it off with remarks like "It's no big deal" or "It's in the past." Friends and spouses can support our healing by reminding us that the abuse against us was, indeed, significant. This kind of encouragement can prevent us from slipping back into denial.

2. Deciding to Heal

Once we admit that our sexual abuse did happen and did indeed scar us, we're ready to face the question "What do I do now?" Awareness of our abuse is only the beginning of freedom from its painful aftermath. This step is the proverbial "fork in the road," and you have to make a choice: healing and restoration or a return to status quo.

Some survivors choose to pretend that everything is fine and take action only when life forces them to go deeper because they're experiencing

+ Painful depression.
+ The breakdown of important relationships.
+ A toxic habit growing out of control.
+ An inability to cope with everyday life.
+ A child leaving home.
+ A daughter entering puberty.

Such circumstances may be the catalyst that helps a person recognize *I can't go on this way. My past is holding me captive.* No matter what brings us to this point, deciding to heal is a powerful and positive choice.

3. Surviving Crisis

At some point your past sexual abuse will crash into your present; this is called the Crisis or Emergency Stage. The day of reckoning eventually comes, that day when the past forces its way into the present and demands to be seen, known, . . . dealt with, and resolved. Memories, or pieces of them, begin to surface during this stage. This happens, in part, because you've made the decision to heal, and your unconscious mind cooperates by releasing your memories. Experiencing memories is a positive sign, demonstrating that you feel safe and secure enough to face them, that you're strong enough to tackle the past. A survivor can't know in advance whether or when this stage will come.

A crisis can be triggered by an event, either positive or negative. You may feel out of control and even fear that you're "going to lose it." If this happens the emotions will feel scary, but disruption and crisis are a normal part of the healing process, and this stage will pass. Believe that, assuring yourself *This will pass.*

You may be approaching the Crisis Stage if

+ *You cry a lot.* Tears may be frequent, uncontrollable, and with no apparent connection to anything currently happening in your life. You may feel highly sensitive.
+ *You feel irritable and angry.* You're touchy, grouchy, and easily annoyed. You're impatient and snap about things that don't usually bother you.
+ *You have strong reactions.* It's normal for a survivor who's entering the healing process to react to certain circumstances with hostility. If your abuser was a man, for example, you may make generalities and manifest anger toward and dislike for all men. You may cry at newscasts when the story of an abused child is in the headlines.

+ *You startle easily.* You're jumpy and easily alarmed.
+ *You withdraw.* You want to isolate yourself and avoid other people. Perhaps your thoughts are often "someplace else." You have a difficult time staying present.
+ *You avoid physical contact.* You want to avoid the hugs, kisses, and physical touches you once allowed.

The above symptoms may be indicators that you're starting to connect with your emotions and trauma. Other disruptions you may experience include:

+ Loss of or excessive appetite.
+ Loss of or excessive sleep.
+ Loss of pleasure in activities you usually enjoy.
+ Loss of or excessive energy expended in normal activities.

4. Remembering

Like the Crisis Stage, which may be defined as the disruptive and fearful stage, the Remembering Stage can be described with two words—*deeply sorrowful*—and can be the longest healing phase for the survivor.

The Remembering Stage goes beyond the memories of abuse to include the process of merging memories and emotions; you remember not only what happened but also *how you felt* during and after the abuse.

In remembering, we refuse to numb ourselves and instead make the deliberate choice to emotionally re-engage. This is an integral part of the healing process.

In the Remembering Stage you may suffer some distressing symptoms, many of which seem to occur randomly and to linger indefinitely. These may include

+ Sleep disorders.
+ Nightmares (or insomnia may be an attempt to escape the torments of recurring dreams).
+ Flashbacks (quick snapshots of the abuse).

+ Heavy clouds of depression.
+ Anger, anxiety, and grief.

The Remembering Stage is also the time when you learn to express your feelings. Because you've been emotionally disconnected, you may be unsure both of what you're feeling and of how to *relay* those feelings in appropriate ways. Seek the encouragement of a helper to give you strength and courage.

5. Choosing to Tell

Survivors don't often share their stories. And when they do talk, it's usually long after the abuse has happened. Only a few people may ever know of the horrors of your childhood. But in this stage you'll discover that telling is a powerful healing force.

Benefits of Telling
+ Receiving support, comfort, and compassion as you relate your story.
+ Deeper intimacy with loved ones.
+ Freedom from denial.
+ Freedom from shame and humiliation as you break secrecy.
+ Encouragement to others to shatter the silence of their abuse.
+ End to isolation and opportunity to build community with other survivors.
+ Self-discovery.

Be prepared, however, for a wide variety of responses during the telling stage, and try to set realistic expectations. Some survivors experience negative, hurtful responses when they share their stories. An individual's reaction to your disclosure may be raw and will be unrehearsed, so ground yourself in the truth.

6. Releasing Responsibility

In this stage you learn to place the responsibility where it belongs—solely on the abuser.

You must choose to believe what *is* true, even if it doesn't *feel* true: the abuse wasn't your fault.

Once you determine that you don't deserve the blame for what happened, you'll need to let go of the excuses you've made to minimize the abuser's responsibility. Assigning responsibility to your abuser also means terminating all former justifications you've made on their behalf. You can no longer reason away your abuser's actions. Doing so in the past has diminished your ability to acknowledge the depth of your wounds, and deeper healing can come only when you have a firm understanding that the crime committed against you was atrocious and is not to be minimized.

7. Finding the Inner Child

Your innocence was savagely stolen, and you've lost touch with your own vulnerability. In this stage you return to your past without cognitive distortions and learn to reconnect to the child within. Here you comfort, soothe, and grieve along with your inner child. You feel her pain. Making contact with the Child Within—showing compassion toward and curiosity about her—can help you feel compassion for the adult you and appropriate anger toward the abuser, as well as increase your capacity for intimacy with others.

8. Grieving Loss

You've sustained many significant losses, yet most survivors don't take the time to name (acknowledge) them, let alone grieve them. In this stage you learn to grieve your losses. By allowing yourself to mourn what has been stolen from you, you honor your pain and find strength to release it.

This stage is accompanied by weeping, and you may feel profound sadness. Don't be alarmed. Unlike the effects of depression, your mourning promotes healing.

While depression is accompanied by a sense of hopelessness and bleak futility, grieving guides you through the passage of pain into freedom on the other side. One favorite Bible verses was especially meaningful to me during this time: "Weeping may remain for a night, but rejoicing comes in the morning" (Psalm 30:5). I like to express it this way: *joy comes with the mourning.* The tears you shed cleanse your soul.

9. Expressing Anger

The Anger Stage is about getting in touch with your intense anger and learning to redirect it in appropriate and therapeutic ways. Until you're willing to release the rage within you and direct it appropriately—toward the abuse, the abuser(s), and the people who failed to protect you—you'll remain stuck. Many therapists have expressed in one way or another that "anger is the backbone of healing." You'll feel empowered when you express your anger, process it, and release it in constructive ways.

10. Forgiveness and Resolution

In this stage you choose to move past your abuse trauma by releasing forgiveness—forgiveness of others, yourself, and God.

In the Resolution Stage you're no longer stuck in the pain of the past. You face your life with anticipation, making substantial strides toward a new and promising future. That's the goal of healing. The Resolution Stage is a time of adventure as you find courage to explore new passions.

This stage is also a time of integration. As you discover God's intentional design for your life, the child within you begins to merge with your adult woman to create the beautiful and unique composite individual that is *you*. In resolution you find peace and discover that you truly aren't responsible for your abuse.

During this stage you may want to confront your abuser; however, not every survivor chooses to take this step. Don't feel forced to face your perpetrator. Your healing doesn't hinge on confrontation.

PRAYER OF WORTH AND VALUE

Jesus, Lord and Friend,

You are the giver of peace. You are the Jesus of joy, the friend of the broken-hearted. I can come to you without fear or shame. I can boldly enter into your throne room without guilt or condemnation because of your cleansing and healing.

You are the One who makes all things new. And you have made me know this newness. You have washed my wounds with your love and softened my scars with the oil of your Holy Spirit.

I am new.

I am your child.

I am the beautiful work of your hands. Hands that are gentle. Hands that are loving and holy. Your hands heal—when they reach out to touch me they bring power and strength. Your touch is comforting and healing, not destructive or demeaning.

You have given me dignity and honor. And I walk in my God-given identity this day and every day. Amen.

— Appendix 3 —

MEN'S CONFESSION OF ABUSE

Instructions: This exercise is designed to be done in partnership with a trusted male whose role it will be to read the statements to you as a representative of the male figure(s) in your life who have wounded and betrayed you sexually. While this exercise is for your healing, it can also be powerfully moving for the man who participates. The activity is included so you can receive an acknowledgment of the significance and scope of your abuse from a male, helping you to move forward toward healing.

As an additional resource I highly recommend *The Apology*, written by my good friend, Dove Award winner, and Christian Songwriter of the Year Steve Siler, the founder and CEO of MusicForTheSoul.org. You can find *The Apology* at MusicForTheSoul.org—Resources—The Apology.

As a FATHER:

+ We failed to protect you.
+ We failed to give you a clear picture of our Father God.
+ We abandoned our post as spiritual leader in our family.
+ We devalued your femininity by wishing you were a boy and treating you like a boy.
+ We weren't as proud of you or of your accomplishments as we were of your brothers'.
+ We used our strength to overpower you physically and emotionally.
+ We crossed sexual boundaries and degraded you.

As a BROTHER:

+ We failed to protect and uphold your honor.
+ We used our physical strength to overpower you.
+ We thought of ourselves as superior to you because of your gender.

As a BOYFRIEND:

+ We told you that you were someone special, but when you saw us hanging around our male friends we ignored you.
+ We based your value on how you looked and viewed you as a sex object.
+ We leered at and demeaned you with sexual innuendos.
+ We ignored you because you didn't live up to our standard of physical appearance.
+ We pressured you to give us something that should have been saved for marriage. Once you gave it, we despised you.
+ We painfully violated your trust by forcing ourselves on you and stripping away your ability to trust.
+ We viewed you as a sexual conquest, and then we bragged about that conquest.
+ We said that we loved you only so we could possess your body for our pleasure. Then we abandoned you and forced you to take the life of your unborn child.

As a HUSBAND:

+ We made promises and then broke them.
+ We overpowered you with our strength and forced our will on you.
+ We failed to value your intuitive thinking and vaunted our own logical thinking.
+ We threatened abandonment in order to get our way.
+ We left you in silence to deal, alone, with your pain.
+ We invested emotionally in relationships outside our marriage and ignored your needs.
+ We pressured you to always be beautiful, to perform flawlessly, and to be perfect.
+ We forced you to function as both mom and dad by valuing our sports, careers, and hobbies over our families.
+ We devalued you by making you live up to airbrushed images of pornography.
+ We expected you to meet all of our needs and desires.

As a BOSS:

+ We overlooked you for promotions because of your gender.
+ We kept you out of the "old boy's club."
+ We pressured you for sexual favors or forced you to accept flirting and innuendo.
+ We despised and rejected your ideas and then took credit for those ideas ourselves.
+ We ignored the obvious reality that these things were going on.
+ We downplayed your significance and contributions.

As a SPIRITUAL LEADER:

+ We used the principle of "submission" to justify abusive situations.
+ We denied the full expression of your gifts and calling within the church.
+ We made you feel as though you were a member of a separate, lower class.
+ We judged your motives with suspicion.
+ We exploited you sexually and then covered it up.
+ We failed to express to you that you, too, were created good and in God's own image.

**For these sins we ask you to forgive us
and to release us into God's hands to deal with us.**

FEELINGS AND EMOTIONS VOCABULARY GUIDE

As discussed in chapter 2, this list of emotions was introduced to me when I was in my twenties in the context of a discussion group for survivors, and I found it immensely helpful for identifying my emotions early on in my healing process, as I began to emotionally "thaw."

Pleasant Feelings			
OPEN	HAPPY	ALIVE	GOOD
understanding	great	playful	calm
confident	glad	courageous	peaceful
reliable	joyous	energetic	at ease
easy	lucky	liberated	comfortable
amazed	fortunate	optimistic	pleased
free	delighted	provocative	encouraged
sympathetic	overjoyed	impulsive	clever
interested	gleeful	free	surprised
satisfied	thankful	frisky	content
receptive	important	animated	quiet
accepting	festive	spirited	certain
kind	ecstatic	thrilled	relaxed
	satisfied	wonderful	serene
	glad		free and easy
	cheerful		bright
	sunny		blessed
	merry		reassured
	elated		
	jubilant		

Pleasant Feelings			
LOVE	INTERESTED	POSITIVE	STRONG
loving	concerned	eager	impulsive
considerate	affected	keen	free
affectionate	fascinated	earnest	sure
sensitive	intrigued	intent	certain
tender	absorbed	anxious	rebellious
devoted	inquisitive	inspired	unique
attracted	nosy	determined	dynamic
passionate	snoopy	excited	tenacious
admiration	engrossed	enthusiastic	hardy
warm	curious	bold	secure
touched		brave	
sympathetic		daring	
close		challenged	
loved		optimistic	
comforted		re-enforced	
drawn toward		confident	
		hopeful	
Difficult/Unpleasant Feelings			
ANGRY	DEPRESSED	CONFUSED	HELPLESS
irritated	lousy	upset	incapable
enraged	disappointed	doubtful	alone
hostile	discouraged	uncertain	paralyzed
insulting	ashamed	indecisive	fatigued
sore	powerless	perplexed	useless
annoyed	diminished	embarrassed	inferior
upset	guilty	hesitant	vulnerable
hateful	dissatisfied	shy	empty
unpleasant	miserable	stupefied	forced
offensive	detestable	disillusioned	hesitant
bitter	repugnant	unbelieving	despairing
aggressive	despicable	skeptical	frustrated
resentful	disgusting	distrustful	distressed

Difficult/Unpleasant Feelings			
ANGRY	DEPRESSED	CONFUSED	HELPLESS
inflamed	abominable	misgiving	woeful
provoked	terrible	lost	pathetic
incensed	in despair	unsure	tragic
infuriated	sulky	uneasy	in a stew
cross	bad	pessimistic	dominated
worked up	feeling loss	tense	
boiling			
fuming			
indignant			
INDIFFERENT	AFRAID	HURT	SAD
insensitive	fearful	crushed	tearful
dull	terrified	tormented	sorrowful
nonchalant	suspicious	deprived	pained
neutral	anxious	aching	grieved
reserved	alarmed	tortured	anguished
weary	panicked	dejected	desolate
bored	nervous	rejected	desperate
preoccupied	scared	injured	pessimistic
cold	worried	offended	unhappy
disinterested	frightened	afflicted	lonely
lifeless	timid	humiliated	dismayed
	shaky	victimized	mournful
	restless	heartbroken	
	doubtful	agonized	
	threatened	appalled	
	cowardly		
	quaking	wronged	
	menaced	alienated	
	wary		

UNDERSTANDING YOUR PERSONAL BOUNDARIES

Many counselors suggest that understanding your personal boundaries and outlining your likes and dislikes in these areas will help to define your individualism.

+ **Physical Boundaries.** How much space do you want to establish between yourself and others? How much privacy and/or time do you need for nurture and self-care? With what kinds of affection and touch are you comfortable? Do you feel free to give hugs? To whom and under what circumstances?

+ **Mental Boundaries.** Are you able to apply your own thoughts, beliefs, values, and opinions to yourself, while allowing others to have theirs? Do you know what you believe, and can you hold on to your opinions without being easily persuaded to second-guess or let go of them? Do you become rigid, defensive, or highly emotional if someone else's opinion or believe system differs with yours? If you become argumentative and angry, you may have weak mental boundaries.

+ **Emotional Boundaries.** Do you take responsibility for your own feelings and emotions without blaming others for them? Can you distinguish the difference between being responsible *to* someone and *for* someone? Healthy boundaries prevent you from accepting guilt for another's behavior and choices. Can you allow others to feel angry, sad, rejected, or afraid (or any other negative emotion) without accepting the responsibility to make them happy? Can you engage in relationships while retaining your own, distinct sense of self?

+ **Sexual Boundaries.** How, when, and with whom do you choose to share sexual intimacy? Do you protect yourself and remain within your comfort level regarding touch and affection?
+ **Spiritual Boundaries.** Can you stand for what you believe without being coerced into violating your principles? Do you validate and trust your experiences and relationship with God?
+ **Material Boundaries.** Do you have a solid concept of what it means to have personal belongings? Can you decide what or when to lend, give, sell, or share without feeling pressure or obligation?

If neither you nor your family members are accustomed to setting and accepting boundaries, the concept of implementing them may seem unattainable at first. You may be enticed by voices—your own or others'—to forget the whole idea.

Once you identify your personal boundaries, be prepared—the testing of your boundaries *will* happen—not just once but frequently.

So what will you do?

Here are some tips:

Clarify the Boundary. Make sure the person understands the boundary you have set. You can do this by asking whether they remember the discussion you had with them about the behavior in question. If they say no, remind them of it and decide whether you're willing to extend grace and offer a second chance with a defined consequence. If not, stick to your guns and follow through.

Follow Through. If a boundary has been violated, make sure to follow through with the predetermined, pre-stated consequence. Remember that a clearly defined boundary must be accompanied by a promised action (consequence) from you if it is ignored or broken. Your follow-through is essential; your willingness to act on your stated intention may result in the difference between remaining in a dysfunctional relationship and a miraculous breakthrough to freedom.

Trust Yourself. If you've set a boundary that seems reasonable and valuable, stick to it. Don't re-evaluate your motives when you're under stress or duress. You'll only end up feeling frustrated and angry at the disrespect shown you. Leave the boundary intact and apply your skill of saying—and meaning—*No! Honor yourself* by reinforcing the wise and healthy decision you've made on your own behalf. You deserve respect.

Change Your Mind. Over time both people and circumstances can change. You will change, others will change, and your situation will probably change. It's fine to adjust a boundary and adapt it to your new normal. Just be certain you're adjusting to your new *healthy* behavior and not accommodating the unhealthy behavior of yourself or of someone else.

EIGHT WAYS TO IMPROVE YOUR BODY IMAGE

+ Appreciate all that your body does for you.
+ Write down a positive declaration that affirms each part of your body.
+ Say "I am beautiful" aloud every day, bearing in mind that beauty is more than skin deep. It's just as fully a matter of mind and spirit.
+ Silence the voices that tell you your body is dirty, bad, ugly, or unacceptable.
+ Honor your body, giving yourself the best food, exercise, and sleep you possibly can.
+ Pay attention to false images of perfection in social media, and reject shallow messages.
+ Treat yourself to something special that shows appreciation for your body.
+ Refuse to abuse yourself. Love your body and tell it often that it's doing a great job for you!

— Appendix 7 —

THE BENEFITS OF FORGIVENESS

Forgiveness benefits you in many ways. It

+ *Leads to inner peace.* You can be free from the torment of your past.
+ *Removes roadblocks in relationships with other people and with God.* Your compassion and empathy for others is restored through forgiveness. Forgiveness allows you to love more fully.
+ *Decreases your level of anger.* It also lessens the likelihood that your anger will be misdirected toward the innocent.
+ *Frees you from the sadness and depression that result from bitterness.*
+ *Releases you from the power that both the offense and the offender have been holding over you.* You're in charge of your attitude and outlook—you're no longer enslaved by the actions of another.
+ *Offers closure from the past because you're investing your emotional energy positively.* Instead of remembering and continuously revisiting the horrors of the past, you're freed to focus on a bright and joyful future.

The beauty of forgiveness frees prisoners—like you and me.

— Appendix 8 —

PRAYER OF WARFARE

Father, I come before You in the name of Your Son, Jesus Christ, who has given me the right to use His authority (Luke 10:19). I push back the powers of darkness and declare in His name that Satan has no right to my family, my possessions, or myself (Mark 16:17–19). I cover the doorposts of my mind, heart, and body with the blood of Jesus, an obstacle that death and destruction are powerless to "pass over." I claim Your divine protection, Lord, and thank You, Jesus, for your wall of angels around me (Psalm 9).

Your Word declares that You "have not given us a spirit of fear, but of power, love and a sound mind" (2 Timothy 1:7). In Jesus' name I bind fear, and I stand on Your Word, which says that if I humble myself before You and resist the devil, he has no choice but to flee (James 4:7). Therefore, the enemy's schemes fall powerless at my feet, and I declare that I will walk through this healing journey with love and with a sound mind. I claim my freedom and wholeness, again in His name (Galatians 5:1).

I thank You in advance. In Jesus' mighty name, Amen.

SENSATE FOCUS

What does sexual intimacy look like? Therapists and even descriptions from the Old Testament book of Song of Solomon describe intimacy as the relationship exemplified by two partners who maintain eye contact and face-to-face orientation, who feel free to exchange uncertainty about themselves as relationship partners, and who love one another deeply and selflessly.

Overview: The Stanford School of Medicine recommends an approach to growing in intimacy known as Sensate Focus, a six-week series of activities that helps couples ease into intimacy without fear of rejection or embarrassment. During the first two weeks both subjects explore the body and face, avoiding erogenous zones such as the breasts and genitalia. The two become closer by exploring touch without experiencing the pressure of expectation to achieve intercourse or orgasm. During weeks two to four non-intercourse stimulation is permitted. Couples are encouraged to be vocal about what they like and dislike as each becomes more comfortable with their partner. In the last two weeks intercourse is allowed, as partners have become ready to take intimacy to a deeper level.

Goal: The goal of Sensate Focus is to build trust and intimacy within your relationship, helping you as partners to give and receive pleasure. The technique emphasizes positive emotions, physical feelings, and responses, while reducing negative reactions.

The Program: The program can help participants overcome previous fears of failure and build more satisfying sexual relationships. Sensate Focus teaches continuous reinforcement as a tool to help couples overcome negative reactions to intimacy.

Ground Rules:

+ Select an agreed-upon, acceptable time and place where you won't be disturbed.
+ Choose pleasant surroundings, selecting music, lighting, and scents that please you.
+ Turn off all phones and, if necessary, lock the door.
+ Take turns giving and receiving touch, allowing each partner equal time.
+ Take your time and enjoy the experience rather than focusing on a goal.
+ Take as long as you want, moving to the next stage when both partners agree.
+ Take plenty of time to explore the other person's body. Experiment with different sensations and types of touch. Take pleasure in experiencing the texture, form, and temperature of the other person's body.
+ Explore the degrees of pressure and types of touch your partner finds most pleasurable by encouraging feedback or placing your hand under theirs so they can guide you.
+ Let your partner know what you do and don't like. You can tell them, make appreciative noises, or guide their hand.
+ Avoid saying "Don't," as this can be discouraging. Instead, make positive suggestions.
+ It may be helpful to talk about the experience afterward. For instance, "I especially liked it when you . . . "
+ Don't be afraid to suggest ideas you'd like to try.

Phase 1: Non-Genital Sensate Focus Ground Rules

+ Feel free to be naked, wear underwear, or wear relaxed clothing— whatever feels most comfortable to you.
+ If you're interested in learning massage techniques, you may find a book or DVD on the topic helpful.
+ At this stage, avoid touching obvious erogenous zones: breasts, nipples, vulva, clitoris, vagina, penis, or testicles.

- Move from one stage to the next only when you both feel comfortable.
- Sexual intercourse and orgasm are not permitted during this phase.

Instructions:

- During these early sessions concentrate on touching visible parts of the body: hands, arms, feet, scalp, and face.
- When you feel comfortable, include the back, neck, arms, buttocks, and legs, still including the hands, feet, and face.
- Finally, include the chest, stomach, shoulders, and thighs, but avoid the breasts, tops of legs, and groin area.

Phase 2: Genital Sensate Focus Ground Rules:

- Now that you've grown comfortable with touch, the time has come to acclimate to touching the breast and genital areas. Spend some time exploring this stage before moving on to the next.
- Continue to pay attention to parts of the body you explored in previous sessions, as well as to new areas.
- Focus on increasing your partner's pleasure, as well as their awareness of your responses to different types of stimulation. It's fine if either of you becomes aroused, but arousal isn't the aim of the exercise.
- Water-based lubricants can be useful during genital stimulation. Oil-based products shouldn't be used with condoms.
- Sexual intercourse/penetration isn't permitted during this phase.

Instructions:

- Incorporate touching of breasts and nipples. Remember that men have nipples, too.
- Next, include the areas around the genitals, including the man's testicles.
- Introduce touching the genitals (labia, clitoris, and entrance to the vagina on a woman; penis, shaft, and glans on a man).
- You may want to incorporate oral as well as manual touch (kissing, licking, sucking) into both non-genital and genital touching.

+ Another option is the "teasing technique." Manually stimulate your partner's genitals, first gently and then with increasing speed. Rest for a few minutes and then begin again.
+ Orgasm may occur, but that is not the aim of the exercise.

Phase 3: Penetrative Sensate Focus Ground Rules:

+ At this stage begin to include penetration, using fingers, toys, and the penis.
+ Continue to give pleasure to other parts of the body as well.
+ The person being penetrated should control both the depth and the length of time of penetration.
+ Orgasm and intercourse are permitted in this phase, but this is not the goal. The aim remains to enjoy growing intimacy.

Instructions:

+ Begin with gentle penetration, with little or no thrusting, and enjoy the sensation.
+ Try exchanging top and bottom positions.
+ Next incorporate thrusting, with the person being penetrated in control.
+ You might find it useful at this point to consult books that suggest sexual positions.

— Endnotes —

1 Choi, Charles Q. "Scientist: Maybe Two Snowflakes Are Alike." LiveScience. January 19, 2007. Accessed April 13, 2016. http://www.livescience.com/1239-scientist-snowflakes-alike.html.

2 UCSB ScienceLine. University of Santa Barbara, California. Web. 19 Apr. 2016.

3 "History of the Four Temperaments." CatholicMatch Institute. Accessed April 19, 2016. http://www.catholicmatch.com/institute/temperaments/history-of-the-four-temperaments/.

4 Munro, Kali. "What to Do with Your Feelings." Toronto Therapy and Online Counseling. Accessed April 18, 2019. kalimunro.com/wp/articles-info/...feelings/what-to-do-with-your-feelings.

5 Cloud, Henry, and John Townsend. *Boundaries: When to Say Yes, How to Say No.* Grand Rapids, MI: Zondervan, 1992.

6 "Naomi—Definition and Meaning, Bible Dictionary." Bible Study Tools. Accessed April 19, 2016. http://www.biblestudytools.com/dictionary/naomi/.

7 "Step Four: Made a Searching and Fearless Moral Inventory of Ourselves." Accessed April 19, 2016. http://www.aa.org/assets/en_US/en_step4.pdf.

8 "Shame." Accessed April 19, 2016. http://www.dictionary.com/browse/shame.

9 Stolorow, Robert D., Ph.D. "The Shame Family: Many Emotional States Have Shame at Their Core." *Psychology Today.* October 4, 2014. Accessed April 19, 2019.

10 Bolton, Jane, Psy.D., M.F.T. "What We Get Wrong about Shame." *Psychology Today.* May 18, 2009. Accessed April 19, 2016. https://www.psychologytoday.com/blog/your-zesty-self/200905/what-we-get-wrong-about-shame.

11 Stolorow, Robert D., Ph.D. "The Shame Family: Many Emotional States Have Shame at Their Core." *Psychology Today.* October 4, 2014. Accessed April 19, 2019. https://www.psychologytoday.com/blog/feeling-relating-existing/201310/the-shame-family.

12 Ledford, Terry L., Ph.D. "Silencing the Internal Critic." World of Psychology. Accessed April 19, 2016. http://psychcentral.com/blog/archives/2015/02/16/silencing-the-internal-critic/.

13 Ledford, Terry L., Ph.D. "Silencing the Internal Critic." World of Psychology. Accessed April 19, 2016. http://psychcentral.com/blog/archives/2015/02/16/silencing-the-internal-critic/.

14 "Emotional and Psychological Trauma." HelpGuide.org. Accessed April 19, 2019. http://www.helpguide.org/articles/ptsd-trauma/emotional-and-psychological-trauma.htm.

15 Heitritter, Lynn, and Jeanette Vought, "Through the Eyes of a Child Victim," in *Helping Victims of Sexual Abuse: A Sensitive, Biblical Guide for Counselors, Victims, and Families.* Minneapolis: Bethany House, 1989, p. 30.

16 Cameron, Sue. *Hope, Healing, and Help for Survivors of Sexual Abuse: A Faith-Based Journey to Healing.* Basingstoke, England: GSC Publishing, 2012.

17 "Strategies for Good Mental Health Wellness." Mental Health Wellness Week. Accessed April 17, 2016. http://www.mhww.org/strategies.html.

18 "Women, Trauma, and PTSD." National Center for PTSD. Accessed April 17, 2019. http://www.ptsd.va.gov/public/PTSD-overview/women/women-trauma-and-ptsd.asp.

19 "Women, Trauma, and PTSD." U.S. Department of Veteran Affairs: National Center for PTSD. Web. http://www.ptsd.va.gov/public/PTSD-overview/women/women-trauma-and-ptsd.asp

20 Herman, Judith Lewis. *Trauma and Recovery*. New York: Basic Books, 2015.

21 Murphy, Cecil. *When a Man You Love Was Abused*. Grand Rapids, MI: Kregel Publications, 2010.

22 Walker, Peter, M.A., M.F.T. "13 Steps for Managing Flashbacks." Peter Walker, M.A., M.F.T. Web. 17 Apr. 2016.

23 "What Is a Dissociative Disorder?" Sidran Institute, http://www.sidran.org/sub.cfm?contentID=75&sectionid=4.

24 "Child Abuse Facts." Safe Horizons. Web. 18 Apr. 2016.

25 Heitritter, Lynne, and Jeanette Vought, "Through the Eyes of a Child Victim," in *Helping Victims of Sexual Abuse: A Sensitive, Biblical Guide for Counselors, Victims, and Families*. Minneapolis: Bethany House, 1989, p. 30.

26 Heitritter, Lynne, and Jeanette Vought, "Through the Eyes of a Child Victim," in *Helping Victims of Sexual Abuse: A Sensitive, Biblical Guide for Counselors, Victims, and Families*. Minneapolis: Bethany House, 1989, p. 30.

27 Correy, Barbara. "The Painful Legacy of Witnessing Domestic Violence." http://bit.ly/mJiJPh.

28 Personal interview May 10, 2017.

29 Personal interview February 5, 2016.

30 McGee, Robert S. "Introduction. Chapters 3–10," in *The Search for Significance, Seeing Your True Worth Through God's Eyes*. Nashville: W Publishing Group, 1998, 2003, p. 26.

31 Johnson, Lorie. "The Deadly Consequences of Unforgiveness." CBN News: The Christian Perspective. CNN, 22 June 2015. Web. 4 Apr. 2016.

32 Brown, Brene. *Rising Strong*. Random House Publishing Group 2015-08-25. Kindle Locations 795-798. Kindle Edition.

33 Cantrell, Julie. *Into the Free*. Harper Collins Publishing 2012, Ch. 40.

— *Acknowledgments* —

Let gratitude be the pillow upon which you kneel to say your nightly prayer. And let faith be the bridge you build to overcome evil and welcome good. —MAYA ANGELOU, Celebrations: Rituals of Peace and Prayer

To my husband, Paul Damon: you are my forever. Your support, strength, and incredible love have changed me. You're proof that soul mates really do exist and that true love really is divinely possible.

To Shelly Jean Beach: your indomitable spirit inspires me. Thanks for your wise counsel and mentorship—not to mention your mad skills as an editor—that have helped make this an excellent resource for help and healing. You're the awesomest (*I hope that's a word*).

To Tim Beals, my publisher, who believed in this book and helped keep my dream alive.

To my many friends and family who loved and supported me through this emotional and vulnerable process. To you, dear Wanda Sanchez.

To my children, Kyle and Lisa Kelley, John and Angela Brooks, Tony and Amber Jones, Ross Damon, and Trent Damon. When I see your beautiful lives, you show me how faithful God is in spite of who we are!

To Terry Jones: Jesus truly is a healer, isn't he? Thank you.

True forgiveness is when you can say, "Thank you for that experience."
—OPRAH WINFREY

Special thanks to my Lord and Savior, Jesus Christ. You have made all things well, and I am truly grateful for You, Jesus!

For over twenty-five years, God has used Dawn Scott Damon to touch people through her personal testimony, her humor, and her writing. She is the author of *When a Woman You Love Was Abused: A Husband's Guide to Helping Her Overcome Childhood Sexual Molestation* (Kregel 2012). Her writing has also appeared in *Charisma Magazine, Light and Life, Spiritled Woman Power Up,* as well as *The Grandmother's Bible* (Zondervan 2008) and *NIV Hope in the Mourning Bible* (Zondervan 2013).

She is a national speaker who has been featured at numerous conferences, including "The Freedom Girl Sisterhood," a national women's conference she founded. Dawn's past challenges have deepened and enriched her ministry, enabling her to understand, empower, and inspire others toward freedom and wholeness. Many hurting people have received healing through Dawn's teaching and story of inner healing.

Dawn is an ordained minister and is pastor and lead spiritual architect of Tribes Church, tribeschurch.tv. She and her husband, Paul, reside in the Grand Rapids, Michigan, area.

For more information on Dawn, visit her at dawnscottdamon.com and freedomgirlsisterhood.com.